T0003388

Cambridge Elements ≡

Elements in Publishing and Book Culture
edited by
Samantha Rayner
University College London
Leah Tether
University of Bristol

PUBLISHING SCHOLARLY EDITIONS

Archives, Computing, and Experience

Christopher Ohge
School of Advanced Study, University of London

CAMBRIDGE
UNIVERSITY PRESS

CAMBRIDGE
UNIVERSITY PRESS

University Printing House, Cambridge CB2 8BS, United Kingdom

One Liberty Plaza, 20th Floor, New York, NY 10006, USA

477 Williamstown Road, Port Melbourne, VIC 3207, Australia

314–321, 3rd Floor, Plot 3, Splendor Forum, Jasola District Centre,
New Delhi – 110025, India

103 Penang Road, #05–06/07, Visioncrest Commercial, Singapore 238467

Cambridge University Press is part of the University of Cambridge.

It furthers the University's mission by disseminating knowledge in the pursuit of
education, learning, and research at the highest international levels of excellence.

www.cambridge.org
Information on this title: www.cambridge.org/9781108720182
DOI: 10.1017/9781108766739

© Christopher Ohge 2021

First published 2021

A catalogue record for this publication is available from the British Library.

ISBN 978-1-108-72018-2 Paperback
ISSN 2514-8524 (online)
ISSN 2514-8516 (print)

Publishing Scholarly Editions

Archives, Computing, and Experience

Elements in Publishing and Book Culture

DOI: 10.1017/9781108766739

First published online: November 2021

Christopher Ohge

School of Advanced Study, University of London

Author for correspondence: Christopher Ohge, christopher.ohge@sas.ac.uk

ABSTRACT: *Publishing Scholarly Editions* offers new intellectual tools for publishing digital editions that bring readers closer to the experimental practices of literature, editing, and reading. After the Introduction (Section 1), Sections 2 and 3 frame intentionality and data analysis as intersubjective, interrelated, and illustrative of experience-as-experimentation. These ideas are demonstrated in two editorial exhibitions of nineteenth-century works: Herman Melville's *Billy Budd, Sailor*, and the anti-slavery anthology *The Bow in the Cloud*, edited by Mary Anne Rawson. Section 4 uses pragmatism to rethink editorial principles and data modelling, arguing for a broader conception of the edition rooted in data collections and multimedia experience. The Conclusion (Section 5) draws attention to the challenges of publishing digital editions, and why digital editions have failed to be supported by the publishing industry. If publications are conceived as pragmatic inventions based on reliable, open-access data collections, then editing can embrace the critical, aesthetic, and experimental affordances of editions of experience.

KEYWORDS: textual scholarship, digital humanities, digital publishing, book history, nineteenth-century literature

ISBNs: 9781108720182 (PB), 9781108766739 (OC)

ISSNs: 2514-8524 (online), 2514-8516 (print)

Contents

1 Introduction

1.1 Textual Histories, Editorial Practices

Textual scholarship is concerned with how texts have been made since the invention of writing. Editions evolve out of a variety of situations and needs: the discovery of a Latin inscription of political graffiti in a buried Roman stone façade, or a newly found manuscript copy of a poem, or a draft manuscript or typescript of a novel, or the discovery of a cache of unpublished letters and notebooks that a historically significant person has left behind. These cannot be read until an editor *prepares* accurate texts and creates varieties of *apparatus* (e.g., introductions, notes, glossaries) to help readers understand the ways in which the texts were made and understood. Such editorial activities consist of layers of analysis and decisions. Every text comes with a history, as well as a collection of puzzles that illuminate an author's creative process, a publishing history, or the text's historical context.

The discipline of scholarly editing has long operated under Samuel Johnson's principle that it serves to 'correct what is corrupt, and to explain what is obscure' and A. E. Housman's definition of it as the 'science of discovering error in texts and the art of removing it'. Editing can now do better than correction by also embracing a creative-critical mode of experimentation and invention. Like Housman, John Dewey held that 'science is an art', but he also promoted a continuity between creative practices and critical appreciation, suggesting a focus on theories and practices 'which are full of enjoyed meanings'.[1] The editorial acts of transcribing, annotating, and organising and designing editions shape 'enjoyed meanings', but they can feel as much like creative as critical activities.

Studying Herman Melville introduced me to scholarly editing and textual studies. Textual scholarship taught me to read carefully and to engage with histories of the creative process and the making of books. While I learned that Melville's marginalia in his books offered enigmatic forms of pre-writing for works such as *Moby-Dick* for which no manuscript survives, I was also working with a team to edit a digital surrogate of one of

---

[1] Housman, 'The Application of Thought to Textual Criticism', p. 68; Dewey, 'Experience, Nature and Art', in Menand (ed.), *Pragmatism: A Reader*, p. 236.

the books that he read and annotated during its composition – Nathaniel Hawthorne's short story collection *Mosses from an Old Manse* (1846) – for Melville's Marginalia Online (http://melvillesmarginalia.org/). Apart from his first book *Typee*, his late poems, and his final novella *Billy Budd, Sailor*, little original evidence of his composition process survives, so many mysteries remain for the editor of Melville.[2] When *Moby-Dick* was published in 1851, for example, Melville issued two books for two different audiences: an American audience that read *Moby-Dick; or, the Whale*, and a British one that read *The Whale*. Melville had decided to hire a private printer to set the type, produce stereotype plates, and print proof sheets for the first American edition, published by Harper & Brothers. He sent those proof sheets to the British publisher Richard Bentley, with additional revisions to the text. Since Melville had considerable control over the wording of his book until he handed it over to his British publisher, modern editors tend to prefer the authority of the first American edition. The British edition has an additional dimension of authority because it includes further revisions by Melville, despite substantive changes made by the publisher regarding its coarse language, homoerotic scenes, anti-monarchical views, and blasphemous passages. The British edition also accidentally left out the epilogue, in which Ishmael explains that he was the only member of the *Pequod* to survive, and moved the opening section of epigraphs called 'Extracts' to the end of the book. The absence of Melville's manuscript or printer's proof sheets means that the editor must guess which changes in the British edition were Melville's and which were made by the publisher. In the cases of censorship, the answer is obvious, but in some other cases it is difficult to know who the reviser is.

Sometimes a single word changes everything. In chapter 132, 'The Symphony', when Captain Ahab delivers a monologue on the nature of his revenge against the White Whale before engaging in his final hunt, he asks, in the first American edition:

---

[2] For more on the *Typee* manuscript fragment, as well as its fascinating publication history, see '*Typee* Manuscript Fragment', in Melville, *Billy Budd, Sailor and Other Uncompleted Writings*, pp. 936–72; Bryant, *Melville Unfolding*; 'Historical Note' in Melville, *Typee*, pp. 277–85. In Exhibition 1, Chapter 2, I examine *Billy Budd* in more detail.

> Is Ahab, Ahab? Is it I, God, or who, that lifts this arm? But if
> the great sun move not of himself; but is as an errand-boy in
> heaven; nor one single star can revolve, but by some invi-
> sible power; how then can this one small heart beat; this one
> small brain think thoughts; unless God does that beating,
> does that thinking, does that living, and not I.

The British edition begins that first sentence, 'Is it Ahab, Ahab? . . .'. By adding 'it', the British edition matches the syntax with its previous and subsequent sentences, 'What is it' and 'Is it I, God . . . ?'. 'Is it Ahab, Ahab?' changes the meaning of the original 'Is Ahab, Ahab?'. In the American version, he is doubting his own identity, whereas in the British he seems to be asking himself about an 'inscrutable' aspect of his agency which may be inauthentic or influenced by innate depravity. Did Melville or the British publisher make that change? Or is it a printer's error with a meaning of some sort? How does the editor decide which phrase to print, and on what grounds?

It is impossible to know whether Melville added 'it' to the British version. The standard Northwestern-Newberry (NN) edition (1988) printed the reading from the first American edition ('Is Ahab, Ahab?'), which is its 'copy text' (or the authoritative base text from which the edition is produced). NN creates an 'eclectic' reading text by emending its American copy text with British variants or conjectures about Melville's final intentions. The NN edition discusses the crux in the textual apparatus in the back of the book, and readers will not know about it unless they happen to find it. The Melville Electronic Library (MEL) digital edition, on the other hand, also uses the first American edition reading in the 'base version' of its *Moby-Dick* reading text. In the spirit of its print prototype, namely, John Bryant and Haskell Springer's Longman Critical Edition of *Moby-Dick* (2009), MEL gives immediate access to the crux and high-lights the problem – and its attendant critical consequences – of the American and British versions in its 'revision narrative' notes. NN and MEL both show the American 'Is Ahab, Ahab?' in their reading texts, but for different reasons.

In another instance, from Melville's Civil War poetry collection, *Battle-Pieces and Aspects of the War* (1866), editors may disagree on the crucial last line of one of his best-known poems, 'The March into Virginia', which concerns the Union's surprising defeat at the First Battle of Bull Run (or First Manassas) in July 1861. Many readers of the poem will see the final stanza rendered this way:

> But some who this blithe mood present,
>> As on in lightsome files they fare,
> Shall die experienced ere three days are spent –
>> Perish, enlightened by the vollied glare;
> Or shame survive, and, like to adamant,
>> Thy after shock, Manassas, share.

However, the first edition of the poem, as well as many other subsequent print and online versions, shows a different final line: 'The throe of Second Manassas share'. The last line is different because Melville revised it in one of his post-publication copies of *Battle-Pieces*, so scholarly editors have determined that Melville's change of mind, after publication, should be respected as a 'final intention' in a reliable, authoritative text. Hence the reading above of 'Thy after shock, Manassas, share'. But it is not that simple. Two of Melville's post-publication copies of the poem, now identified as Copy A and Copy C, show two different revision processes, as Figure 1 shows.

In one revision sequence (Copy A), Melville seeks to fix the parallelism in the last stanza of 'But some who this blithe mood present' with 'Or some survive' (to replace the original 'Or shame survive'). The substitution of 'some' for 'shame' changes the meaning of the line to focus on the survivors of the battle rather than an abstract sense of shame. In a separate sequence (in Copy C), Melville did not make that some/shame substitution but revised the last line of the poem. He first tried 'Manassas' second throe and deadlier share' – using the possessive of 'Manassas' second throe' to foreshadow the second battle of Manassas (29–30 August 1862), which was an even worse defeat for the Union. He then inscribed a new line, 'Thy second shock, Manassas, share', before settling on 'Thy after shock,

Figure 1 'The March into Virginia', in two of Melville's post-publication copies of *Battle-Pieces and Aspects of the War* (1866): on the left, his bound copy of the first edition (Copy A), with a single pencil revision in the penultimate line of the last stanza; on the right, his custom-bound set of printer's sheets (Copy C), with revisions in the third and sixth lines of the last stanza. Houghton Library, Harvard *AC85 M4977 866b (A) and AC85 M4977 866b (C). Also available in MEL at https://melville.electroniclibrary.org/battle-pieces-corrected-first-edition-and-bound-proofs.

Manassas, share' – again changing the meaning and the meter of the poem's ending. He also considered substituting 'three days be spent' for 'three days are spent'. But the question mark in the right margin between the two revisions in Copy C could indicate a continuing puzzlement or dissatisfaction with the last line.

Editors of *Battle-Pieces* need to address multiple questions for this poem: do they print both texts side-by-side, ignore the post-publication revisions as tentative or incomplete tinkering and just edit the first edition, create a single reading text that conflates the revisions of both pages in A and C, or consider Melville's more extensive revisions in Copy C to be final and print only those revisions? What is the rationale for each of these editorial choices? And how would an editor explain these textual problems while providing the historical context of the two Civil War battles? These are the kinds of questions whose answers form the basis of editorial principles. What does the evidence suggest about the writing of these texts, and how can technology facilitate a reliable editorial process while opening up the texts to readers for their own intellectual and creative aims? MEL editors chose to present the two images (from Copy A and C), coupled with revision narrative notes in the reading text of *Battle-Pieces*, to offer immediate insights into Melville's creative process and to demonstrate how a sequential set of practices in a digital edition can help readers navigate Melville's composition. The conditions of the writing practice that produced these variant final lines should guide editors in choosing how to present those lines, enabling readers to experience writing and editing as forms of experimentation.

The abiding spirit of this book is what editing *does*, as opposed to what it *is*. Rather than defining concepts or theories, I will demonstrate the significance of *making* editions – the editorial practices and aesthetic affordances of editing works of literature with current technologies.[3] By 'practices' I am alluding to Emerson's dictum to 'reduceth [your] learning to practice',[4] as well as Wittgenstein's late aphorism that '[t]he *practice*

---

[3] Crymble has recently made a similar argument about the practices of historians in *Technology and the Historian*, pp. 7–9, 161–6.

[4] Emerson, 'The Method of Nature', in Cramer (ed.), *The Portable Emerson*, p. 110.

gives words their meaning'.[5] I am also reminded of the poet-scholar Donald Davie:

> The practice of an art
> is to convert all terms
> into the terms of art.[6]

Bringing the pragmatic principle of the 'primacy of practice'[7] to editing means that editors should focus on the interrelated practices of writers, publishers, and editors. As Susan Greenberg has also suggested, these activities inevitably generate historical insights about creation, explanation, appreciation, and interpretation in the making of texts, from composition to publication.[8] A text may merely be a string of characters or digital binary code, or even an idea in one's head, but the intentional practices of writers, readers, and even publishers set the contours of the literary work.[9] And practice is stable insofar as there is sufficient agreement among practitioners to constrain the activities that define it. Grounding intentions and practices in *application* means that editorial rules are fluid, yet they are grounded in important histories. Editing therefore requires training to master such practices, but also self-examination, re-calibrating its relation to its traditions, its concepts, and its resource limitations. When editors consider the options for publication in this burgeoning digital epoch, their self-examination is even more intensified. Editors now need to be earnest – and pragmatic – about what publishing options are available to them.

The word 'edition' comes from the Latin *editio*, which connotes several practical products or *exhibitions*. Editing participates in various traditions of

---

[5] Wittgenstein, *Remarks on Colour*, §317. [6] Davie, 'July, 1964', *Essex Poems*, p. 5.

[7] Putnam, *Pragmatism*, p. 52.

[8] In *A Poetics of Editing*, Greenberg conceives of editing as forward-looking and full of possibilities, rather than being merely the gatekeeper of accuracy. Greenberg's model of *autopoiesis* cuts across practical and scholarly conventions of editorial practice, suggesting that the 'ideal editor' exists in a nexus of author, text, and reader.

[9] Lamarque, 'Wittgenstein, Literature, and the Idea of a Practice', pp. 376–77.

textual transmission and mediation. What the Melville examples show is the constraints not only of mixed version ('eclectic' or 'copy-text') critical editing – which previously had to operate within the limitations of print technology – but also of any insular, top-down theory of editing. Each example given earlier concerns the same author but suggests different practices based on different problems arising from different kinds of documentary evidence. The process inherent in pragmatism leads to principles that can still allow for counter-principles while promoting continuities between a variety of experiences of the text, recalling Christopher Ricks's invocation to use 'hard thinking [that] is resolutely unelaborated beyond the exposition and application of principles'.[10] Digital editing is able to create a workflow for not only books as books, and texts as texts, and texts shaped by books, but also data that can be visualised, queried, networked, shared, and manipulated. Technology facilitates critical engagement with all these different textual conditions, enabling a digital edition or archive to accommodate a variety of approaches: book history, textual and contextual notes, narratives of revision, data analysis, critical interpretation, translation, and creative adaptation.

An editor must begin with questions about preparing texts for publication. Is an editor an arbiter or an archivist of texts? Should editors keep versions of texts intact as they were presented to the public or saved in repositories, or should editors create a new text that is more accurate, readable, or faithful to some conception of the originating writer's intentions? Does a reader enter the edition through a single reading text, with a record of variant wordings, multiple versions of texts, or multiple interfaces? Does the editor see their primary role as explaining textual change, the critical discourse, or the historical significance of the text through contextual notes? The answers will dictate how one prepares, encodes, and publishes the edition, and those decisions need to be situated within the traditions of textual scholarship and bibliography. These traditions, as the great practitioner W. W. Greg put it, fundamentally concern the historical reconstruction of the 'living word' in its material forms,[11] Two questions

---

[10] Ricks, 'In Theory'.

[11] Greg, 'Bibliography: A Retrospect' (1945), quoted in Howard-Hill, 'W. W. Greg as Bibliographer', p. 68.

arise from attempting such reconstructions: which writer, editor, or group of writers and editors is worth attending to, and which stages of creative output merit editorial attention?[12]

Why begin a study of textual editing and technology with an argument for editorial practices? Textual scholarship and bibliography are now neglected in several humanities disciplines, which leaves students lacking in exposure to the fundamental stories of how the making of texts shapes their reading experiences and critical interpretations. In my digital editing workshops and modules, I have noticed many participants caught in a double-bind: they need to be trained in both textual scholarship *and* digital technology. The pressure on many of these courses is to skim over, if not ignore outright, the history and methods of editing and bibliography if only because the tech skills are difficult enough to fill an entire course.[13] On the one hand, many of the nuances about *why* and *under which principles* we edit texts have been overwhelmed by the near-prescriptive digital ethos of *how* to encode texts in computer languages such as XML (extensible markup language), which has given an unfortunate impression that digital editing is mechanical work for 'non-critical' tech workers.[14] On the other hand, the methods of traditional textual editing have become ossified by an uncritical acceptance of abstractions such as 'foul papers', 'accidentals', 'final intention', 'social forces', 'paratext', and, lately, 'data models'. As Paul Werstine has argued, editing ought to apply a critical view towards those concepts and proceed by 'respecting the limits of the documentary evidence in hand'.[15]

[12] See Tanselle, *Rationale of Textual Criticism*, pp. 70–4.

[13] For example, two popular summer courses on TEI XML, at the Digital Humanities Summer Institute and the Oxford Digital Humanities Summer School, typically have not devoted sufficient attention to surveying methods of textual scholarship and bibliography. Their primary aim is technical training.

[14] Earhart, *Traces of the Old, Uses of the New*, p. 34.

[15] Werstine, *Early Modern Playhouse Manuscripts and the Editing of Shakespeare*, pp. 1, 231. See also Olsen-Smith, *The Inscription of Walt Whitman's 'Live Oak, with Moss' Sequence*. Olsen-Smith finds that the shortcoming of Bowers's theory of critical editing of Whitman is 'conceptual rather than methodological' – that is, it is beholden to a dogma of final intention instead of examining the context of

Digital editing and text analysis require a grounding in textual scholarship, by which I mean the historical treatments of texts and accuracy, provenance, editorial design and presentation of texts, and textual and contextual apparatus (or forms of annotation).[16] Textual scholarship is central to the life of several disciplines ranging from literature and music to history and sociology.[17] Despite the spirited editorial debates among practitioners since the inception of philology in the nineteenth century, 'the question has very rarely been which editorial framework was best for the type of document under consideration', as Elena Pierazzo has argued.[18] Digital technology may have increased speed, flexibility, and accessibility, but it has not changed the dynamic nature of textual scholarship itself.[19]

Editors and bibliographers must continue to push their thinking further by experimenting with computing and adopting a pragmatic view towards its principles. Unfortunately, the past twenty years or so of born-digital and hybrid print-digital editing have yielded few editions that do more than books can do. Many editors are still stuck in a document- and codex-oriented mode that expects book reading to translate into screen reading, even though studies have been suggesting that users of digital resources prefer basic and advanced searching for specific information over long-term

Whitman's manuscript revisions and publication process of the *Calamus* poems on their own merits.

[16] For foundational guides to scholarly editing, see Gaskell, *A New Introduction to Bibliography*; Greetham, *Textual Scholarship*; Williams and Abbott, *An Introduction to Bibliographical and Textual Studies*; and Pierazzo, *Digital Scholarly Editing*.

[17] Christopher Ricks and Archie Burnett (and, before him, Geoffrey Hill) made this the operating principle of the Editorial Institute at Boston University: 'the textually sound, contextually annotated edition is central to the life of many disciplines. Its primary aims are the promotion of critical awareness of editorial issues and practices and the provision of training in editorial methods'. See also Jerome McGann's *A New Republic of Letters*, which makes a renewed call for the poetic and critical possibilities of editing.

[18] Pierazzo, *Digital Scholarly Editing*, p. 77.

[19] See Bordalejo, 'Digital versus Analogue Textual Scholarship'.

browsing.[20] A study of practices and evolving principles requires identifying how editors have done their work in the past, what has worked well (and not so well), and how those practices might be used in an editorial project such as any reader of this book might want to undertake.[21] Pragmatism does not mean less work but studying what has worked without the trappings of ideology. To paraphrase Dewey, there can be no theory without a counter-theory, as theory begins when someone expresses doubts about existing theories – a dynamic that Richard Rorty calls 'a bundle of intertwined dialectical sequences'.[22] This reflective theorising is practical and consequential. A pragmatic editor adopts an attitude towards one theory to justify attitudes towards another theory or set of theories. An editor's view towards, say, the theory of socialised text editing cannot be held independently of theories of critical text editing.[23] Textual problems are such that they will always be equally problematic to existing editorial theories. The point is to do the editing and to reflect on it at the same time, and to complement that study of methodological principles with digital experimentation.

1.2 Editions as Pragmatic Inventions

The framing of editorial practices – or thinking of what editions do – illustrates a pragmatic proviso that editions are tools for recovering and shaping cultural heritage. The edition is not only the object of critical attention for scholars and students; it is an invention of the text that consists of other inventions – of truth, an ontology of the literary work in relation to its parts (documents and works and their respective versions), method, and publications. These inventions affect the making and publishing of editions, and they require re-thinking about the role of experience in the digital era. Literary works are real cultural objects that *happen* – they are enacted in the

[20] See, e.g., Crymble, 'Digital Library Search Preferences'.

[21] I make sure to complement training in markup languages with seminars on the traditions of textual editing in my courses at the London Rare Books School and the History of the Book programme at the Institute of English Studies.

[22] Rorty, *Consequences of Pragmatism*, pp. 24–5, 65.

[23] See Greg, 'The Rationale of Copy-Text'; Bowers, *Bibliography and Textual Criticism*; McGann, *A Critique of Modern Textual Criticism*.

world.[24] Any editorial theory in the abstract gets undermined by the reality that each individual text or archive comes with its own particularities, contingencies, and set of demands. Editing is a maker's knowledge, in the tradition of practical reason.

The editor can then reduce doubt through an analysis of what we claim to know about authorial intentions, texts and works, but also information technology and publication workflows. This mode of thinking and modelling grounds textual decisions in warranted claims about concrete evidence and focuses on making appropriate technological decisions for delivering editions for specific uses. Turning away 'from abstraction and insufficiency, from verbal solutions, from bad *a priori* reasons, from fixed principles, closed systems, and pretended absolutes and origins', pragmatists turn 'towards concreteness and adequacy, towards facts, towards action'.[25] This allows editors to think about what principles (which can call upon previous theories) are best employed for the evidence in question. Instead of emphasising a 'theoretical pursuit', editing in the digital era is a *programme for action* towards the coherence of the texts of works under consideration, of collaboration and balance.[26] Such a programme nevertheless requires attention to the role that concepts play in our practices.

What are the *functions* of the concepts of editing – of document, text, work, intention, version, edition, model, interface? What theoretical assumptions about what we know are taken for granted, and how do we make truth claims about texts?[27] How do editors document those decisions as they are preparing texts? It may be tempting to chase editing up the tree of theory, as Quine put it – focusing on concepts as abstract, *a priori* explanatory forces[28] – but the best theories are the ones with the fewest

---

[24] Lamarque, *Work and Object*, pp. 2–4. See also Eggert, *Securing the Past*.

[25] James, 'What Pragmatism Means', in Menand (ed.), *Pragmatism: A Reader*, p. 97

[26] 'The knower is an actor, and coefficient of the truth on one side, while on the other he registers the truth which he helps to create' (James, 'Spencer's Definition of Mind as Correspondence', quoted in Putnam, *Pragmatism*, p. 17).

[27] See Craig, *Knowledge and the State of Nature*.

[28] Quine, *Philosophy of Logic*, p. 35.

metaphysical commitments, or the simplest explanations or models with the least unwarranted, or ad hoc, assumptions. Editors need not multiply concepts beyond what is necessary to make useful editions, nor should they be seduced by concepts 'governing' their enterprise.[29] Ideas are tools, as Rorty emphasised, so editing requires an analysis of how different cultural forms fit with their intended functions. I have yet to see a theory that works well for every textual situation and experience.

Many difficult debates arise in editing because of a conflation between the projects of pure and practical inquiry. A traditional textual scholar was tempted to join the purist in finding truth and *eliminating* error, by pursuing final intentions and smoothing over the presumed vagaries of text transmission. The practical inquirer balances 'our need for truth (and the avoidance of error) with the constraints and limitations that we fallible humans encounter in daily life', to quote Michael Hannon.[30] Both the pure and the practical inquirer want to maximise truth claims, but the purist wants to admit no room for error. The practical inquirer is what is called by philosophers a fallibilist – striving for reliability in the pursuit of verifiable options, yet open to the possibility of contingencies and error. Anthony Grafton has recently shown in his book *Inky Fingers* that even in the early modern era of hand-press printing, writers, readers, 'castigators' (correctors), and printers accepted both that the process of collaboration would improve the work and that errors would make their way into the texts. In textual editing, truth is constrained by the contingencies of the writing process, not only from the evidence of authorial composition – such as surviving manuscripts, external testimony of the author's wishes, the available print record, and textual commentaries – and the original publishing process but also from the editor's working conditions, staff, funding, publishing house, and career circumstances.

My pragmatic approach to editing is indebted to Samuel Johnson's editorial maxims to correct what is corrupt, to clarify what is obscure, but

---

[29] Audi (ed.), *The Cambridge Dictionary of Philosophy*, p. 631; Quine, 'On What There Is', in *From a Logical Point of View*, pp. 1–19.

[30] Hannon, *What's the Point of Knowledge?*, p. 219.

also to maintain a 'middle way between presumption and timidity'.[31] Johnson trusted that, with appropriate explication, readers would find their way through the text; he was cautious of conjectural emendations. Pragmatism is not exclusively a word that encompasses a middle-way attitude towards practice and practical success in action; it is also a kind of logic that facilitates 'a method for the analysis of concepts', based in a consideration of what vocabularies are 'good', in terms of generating new meaningful terminologies and modes of explication, and useful.[32] Text making and editing come with indeterminacies – technologies and information access can change quickly, and re-editing must commence as soon as new material, or new perspectives on that material, come to light. A pragmatic method allows us to judge which editorial theories are most appropriate to the material we are interested in, and how that interest itself can be framed in action-oriented, practicable principles.[33]

Instead of staking a claim for an overarching textual theory in place of another, I echo Christopher Ricks's maxim that editors frame their principles in terms of the gains and losses of their decisions. Each decision entails an advantage and a disadvantage, and there is not a single edition (print or digital) that solves a textual crux without some sacrifice. Consider Walter Gropius's Bauhaus design: his house in the woods in Lincoln, Massachusetts, works well because of its interaction with nature, the ways in which the light comes into the rooms at the right times of the day, and, generally, how the architecture follows the principles of Bauhaus design that integrates minimal materials, light, and the natural world. Regardless of one's opinions of Gropius's style, it is hard not to be awed by the economy and charm of the house. Yet it is hard to see the success of Gropius's PanAm

[31] Woudhuysen (ed.), *Samuel Johnson on Shakespeare*, pp. 113 and 159.

[32] Peirce, 'A Definition of Pragmatism', in Menand (ed.), *Pragmatism: A Reader*, pp. 56–7; Rorty, *Consequences of Pragmatism*, p. 142. Greetham also picks up Gerald Graff's view that literary-textual studies constitute not a 'set of systematic principles' but instead 'an inquiry into assumptions, premises, and legitimating principles and concepts' (Gerald Graff, *Professing Literature* (University of Chicago Press, 1987), p. 252, quoted in Greetham, *Theories of the Text*, p. 18).

[33] See, e.g., Ezell, 'Editing Early Modern Women's Manuscripts'.

building on Park Avenue in New York: the Bauhaus aesthetic does not work as a skyscraper in New York City; it works much better as a family home in the woods. The experience is what works. Such an awareness of experience is not merely an argument for atmospherics; it constitutes an argument to move from what Dewey called the 'ready-made compartmentalization' of ideas towards 'a conception that discloses the way in which these works idealize qualities found in common experience'.[34]

Pragmatists are less interested in truth per se than in inquiry – the way we think, how we think, why concepts (good and bad) persist, and where our thinking is taking us. The edition then uses scholarship to strive towards what Charles Sanders Peirce called 'opinion which is fated to be ultimately agreed to by all who investigate'.[35] But there are truths that may never be discovered, as Simon Blackburn has clarified, so the process of inquiry involves the 'actual laborious processes through which we are entitled to take ourselves as getting nearer to the truth'.[36] Pragmatism relies upon a notion of truth 'made largely out of previous truths', and *eventual* verification. Hilary Putnam reframed the goal as an 'idealized rational acceptability', which asks for competence and theoretical and operational constraints.[37] The process of inquiry itself involves the rational practices by which we decide and revise what works. The more open that process is, the better, and that can be done now in the digital space.

The framework of pragmatism allows editors to embrace and build upon the differences of previous editorial theories, to create new practices and tools, and to embrace technology as a means for publication, discovery, and experimentation. My emphasis on experimentation illustrates what John McCarthy and Peter Wright call a 'zestful integration' between aesthetic experience and technology.[38] Borrowing Mikhail Bakhtin's notion of 'creative understanding', McCarthy and Wright's dialogical perspective of technology suggests a relational process of forging understanding through aesthetic activities. This mode of human–computer design increases access,

---

[34] Dewey, *Art as Experience*, p. 10.

[35] Peirce, 'How to Make Our Ideas Clear', quoted in Blackburn, *Truth*, p. 32.

[36] Blackburn, *Truth*, p. 33. [37] Putnam, *Reason, Truth, and History*, p. 55.

[38] McCarthy and Wright, *Technology as Experience*, pp. 17–18, 71–75.

critical nuance, and aesthetic appreciation in digital archives. Editing can get readers as close to the creative process as they can be without being the writer. Pragmatic digital editing goes even further; it reveals the multiplicity of options – or the layers – of the creative process in ways that were never possible with books alone.

Editing is fundamentally grounded in publishing, so it reflects the consensus not just of practitioners in philology, bibliography, and textual scholarship but also of publishers and technologists. Technology has always been at the heart of textual transmission, and it should be a focus of textual scholarship; yet the technological fallacy has also created a false impression that the latest innovations will solve our problems.[39] Technology is born out of developing systems of mediation; it is built by humans who bring their own 'web of beliefs' to systems, or clusters of accepted practices and ideas.[40] This means that technology must be understood in its contexts of development and use; some technologies will not be useful for some types of content.[41] The digital 'edition' comprises the *products* of 'mixed methods': print books, electronic texts, databases, and visualisations – all as complementary tools.[42] Editions no longer need to be simply mechanical, passive products; rather, they can exist as data collections the formats of which provide the impetus for aesthetic experience – that is, experimentation with texts, literary appreciation, deep and interconnected knowledge.[43] Editors now need a plan for creating a computational pipeline that organises these complicated data and metadata of human biases and linguistic eccentricities. A 'computational pipeline' is the model that the editor creates to curate, disseminate, and preserve the scholarly data, which means not only making open-source, non-proprietary, machine-readable data available but also

[39] See Tanselle, 'Print History and Other History'.

[40] See Quine, 'Two Dogmas of Empiricism', in Quine, *From a Logical Point of View*, pp. 20–46.

[41] Thompson, *Books in the Digital Age*, pp. 317–18.

[42] See Sá Pereira, 'Mixed Methodological Digital Humanities'.

[43] Dewey: 'The "eternal" quality of great art is its renewed instrumentality for further consummatory experiences' ('Experience, Nature and Art', in Menand (ed.), *Pragmatism: A Reader*, p. 242).

having a sense of what the project will disseminate (e.g., websites, PDFs, data sets, and so on) with a workflow that matches the project's needs to current publication technologies.[44]

Embracing the ideal of making FAIR (findable, accessible, interoperable, and machine-readable) data available will ensure version control, access, and preservation, which in turn will contribute to the growing collection of Web materials. Yet this ideal inevitably encounters the resource inequalities in academia and publishing, so pragmatism is required to demonstrate both the value and the viability of editing. The computational pipeline that privileges minimal computing principles not only makes for an easier publishing process but also mitigates some of these resource concerns. Using such a computational approach means that files of record can be changed and reflected in various output formats, ranging from print books to websites. Many distinguished scholars still use proprietary word-processing software, and for understandable reasons: the WYSIWYG (what-you-see-is-what-you-get) interface is easy and has helpful tools, and most publishers still require .docx submissions. If the editor's goal is print publication, then that workflow is understandable, but the decision to use only WYSIWYG tools still entails a significant loss of information – not only descriptive markup and metadata but also sharable scholarly data (which I address in Chapter 4). The practice of print-first desktop publishing means that the design and the execution of the edition are constrained by what is possible in a printed book. Any descriptive features cannot be recorded in a word processor; such information, if at all, can visually be only implied for readers of books, whereas encoded digital files enable making explicit that which is implicit in the text.

The pragmatic editor strives to understand the intentional relations between the author's original attempts at writing and publishing and the editor's attempts to understand them and publish reliable texts. All these practices constitute various kinds of know-how that come together in holistic – and fluid – webs of understanding which can be realised in digital

---

[44] The 'computational pipeline' is not my term: David Birnbaum has used it in several editing contexts, including the influential NEH Institute for Advanced Topics in the Digital Humanities that I attended in the summer of 2017.

media. William Empson's principle that, while 'no explanation can be adequate', 'any one valid reason that can be found is worth giving' suggests a self-reflexive framework: 'the more one understands one's own reactions the less one is at their mercy'.[45] Such a principled awareness allows me to make informed judgements about a textual situation based on the surviving documentary evidence and the relevant context, audience, and readerships, without resting on all-encompassing theories. Grounding that framework in pragmatism means that sound critical judgements still require a rich background, discipline, and the ability to discriminate and draw conclusions from available evidence.[46]

My aim in this book is to offer intellectual tools based in a pragmatic tradition that is attentive to experience. 'Experience' may cause suspicion – *experience of what and for whom?* I do not mean experience in the usual sense of perceptual awareness or sense data. Experience is a term that is grounded not only in Emerson's meditative essay of that name from 1844 but also in the classical pragmatists (Charles Sanders Peirce, William James, George Mead, and John Dewey) who rejected mind-object dualisms and abstract concepts in favour of functional accounts of thoughts, feelings, and success in action. Dewey in particular made experience a central concern of his philosophy, and stated that having an aesthetic experience can facilitate 'a transformation of interaction into participation and communication'.[47] As Robert Brandom clarifies, experience entails an experimental circuit of perceiving, acting, identifying the advantages and disadvantages of those actions, and bringing that process to bear on further perceptions.[48] Paul Grimstad extends Brandom's thesis to literature by arguing that experience concerns *composition*, not as a recording of perceptions but as an experimental *process* of literary writing.[49]

Experience is foundational to the nature of textual editing in the digital age; digital editing can bring out the nuances of composition using data and interfaces, demonstrating the relation between experience and experiment,

---

[45] Empson, *Seven Types of Ambiguity*, p. 15.

[46] See Dewey, *Art as Experience*, ch. 13.   [47] Dewey, *Art as Experience*, p. 22.

[48] Brandom, *Between Saying and Doing*, p. 87.

[49] Grimstad, *Experience and Experimental Writing*, pp. 1–2, 12.

and setting the groundwork for deeper knowledge through situated crea-tivity. Through a combination of editorial design, digital images, multi-media formats, and revision narratives, readers can understand how, for example, Melville continued to experiment with *Battle-Pieces* after it was published, or how *Billy Budd* went from being a ballad to a tragic novella. Being immersed in the traces of Melville's composition invites creative modes of reading and new editorial principles. Similarly, Marta Werner's work in print and digital editions of Emily Dickinson has always been grounded in experiential and aesthetic questions of the material documents and compositional process. In her recent edition, *Writing In Time: Emily Dickinson's Master Hours*, Werner combines Dickinson's mysterious 'Master' letters with her epistolary envelope poetry from the same period to evince 'an experiment' that 'seeks a maximum act of attention and detailed focus in order to touch upon the mysteries that these radiant documents both make visible and keep hidden'.[50] Engaging in experience-as-composition, or what Werner calls 'enact[ing] my own metamorphosis from editor to executant', readers can build on their own form of processual experience and open themselves up to having an aesthetic experience of writing.

With these reasons in mind, I begin Chapter 2 with the classic problem of authorial intention in editing and argue for both the primacy of writers' intentions as well as the reciprocal, intersubjective, fluid nature of intentions and experiences that can be realised in digital editions. Exhibition 1 demon-strates these ideas in the digital edition of Herman Melville's *Billy Budd, Sailor*, which I co-edit with John Bryant and Wyn Kelley for MEL. Chapter 3 considers the feedback loops of experiencing data and literary process through encoded texts with analytical aims, resulting in digital editions that can offer a variety of interface experiences ranging from annotated reading texts and linguistic statistics to data analysis and visua-lisations. Exhibition 2, on British activist Mary Anne Rawson's anti-slavery literature anthology *The Bow in the Cloud* (1834), shows how text encoding and text analysis are integrated into an edition that concerns the nexus of manuscripts, book history, and network analysis. Chapter 4 argues for the

---

[50] Werner, *Writing In Time*, p. 11.

continuity between a pragmatic method of editing and the equally pragmatic methods of data modelling and minimal computing principles for publication.

Editorial methodologies used to be dictated by the medium of print. Now digital technology has forced editors to create new methodologies that can facilitate immersions into, and transformations of, texts.[51] As James Smithies has argued, humanities research must use technology 'not only to explain historical events and interpret texts, but to engineer working technical products to do so'.[52] Technical products require publishing mechanisms which need to be resourced. In the Conclusion (Chapter 5) I draw attention to the lack of publishing support for digital editions because the de facto guidelines from the Text Encoding Initiative (TEI) have so far not been adopted by the publishing industry. This is a complicated situation that has no simple solutions. I have been invested in TEI projects (large and small) for nearly twelve years – as the two exhibitions show, my work on Melville and Rawson's anti-slavery anthology uses TEI. Before that, I used TEI for the Mark Twain Project Online, and before that, I published a TEI XML edition of a notebook by the Transcendentalist Christopher Cranch. I have taught – and will continue to teach – TEI at my institution and promote it because I value its pragmatic ethos as well as its ability to record nuanced semantic information and editorial decisions. But the lack of resources and of publication support for TEI projects are significant barriers for many people. A TEI project is worth the investment if it has the expertise and the resources required to build and maintain it. In the absence of those resources, I suggest several promising options for curating and publishing scholarly data using minimal computing, content management platforms, and the International Image Interoperability Framework (IIIF), and by building partnerships with institutional libraries. In bringing pragmatism to bear on both textual editing and technology, I focus less on abstract theories and computational data models and more on what Dewey called the 'movement of thoughts' (i.e., practices and intentional relations) to

---

[51] McCarthy and Wright, *Technology as Experience*, pp. 61–2.

[52] Smithies, *The Digital Humanities and the Digital Modern*, p. 3.

present and foster aesthetic experience.[53] The notion of an edition of experience is an ideal that puts the focus on the networks of intentions among writers, editors, and readers, and digital publications are the sites where these literary and editorial experiments meet. These inventions of the text will generate feedback loops of experience filled with renewed intellectual insights and literary appreciation.

1.3 On the Trouble of Textual Editing

> I watched four curious creatures,
> travelling together; their tracks were swart,
> each imprint very black. The birds' support
> moved swiftly; it flew in the air,
> dived under the wave. The toiling warrior
> worked without pause, pointing the paths
> to all four over the beaten gold.
> —Old English riddle poem (trans. Kevin Crossley-Holland)[54]

The answer to the riddle is digital: not the machine but the technology of the quill and controlled by the fingers (digits). The fingers have the power to launch the *textus receptus* (the text received by the public), itself a strange creature. Gwendolyn Brooks's apt lines in 'To Black Women' to 'Prevail across the editors of the world! / who are obsessed, self-honeying and self-crowned / in the seduced arena' should remind editors to be sceptical of abstract claims such as 'social forces', especially if those forces are sometimes dubious and even, in some cases, oppressive to individual writers who are marginalised in the culture.[55] Scholarly editing can correct past wrongs against authors who were subjected to oppressive forces, whether commercial or cultural. Scholarly editors can and should be mindful of their role as against those 'editors of the world'.

---

[53] Dewey, 'Ralph Waldo Emerson', in *The Philosophy of John Dewey*, p. 25.

[54] Crossley-Holland, *The Exeter Book Riddles*, p. 54.

[55] Brooks, *To Disembark*, p. 44.

It might seem like a paradox that the work of the editor is at once an activity of doing as little as possible to damage the writer's work while changing that text and creating a new one, so editors must strike a careful balance with a text. That tension reinforces the notion that the discipline of editing partakes of change – as D. F. McKenzie puts it, 'change and adaptation are a condition of survival, just as the creative application of texts is a condition of their being read at all'.[56] McKenzie is referring to not only content but also form, material, and apparatus, ranging from contextual to textual treatment of the material, publication design, organisation, and interface.

Editing begins with clarifying or even correcting the textual record, but that can come at a cost. How much detail is necessary in a scholarly edition? Should every variant be recorded, every odd term be glossed, every name be tagged? One is right to wonder about the usefulness of such detail, but every edition is curated, and that curation is the product of judgements contingent upon the limits of the project. As Ricks recently put it: 'Editing, whatever else it may take (imagination, for instance, and conscience, and intellectual curiosity), entails the taking of trouble'.[57] Editors must make decisions. And, regardless of the 'principle and practice' employed, the taking of trouble (of accuracy and tact and intellectual daring) and the promotion of intellectual tensions ought to be prioritised, not avoided.

Editing reveals within texts 'a constantly shifting balance of gains and losses', as Richard Poirier writes.[58] Editing mediates between two forms of experience: the first, between the creative force of the writer's imagination and a learned judgement of what that writer intended; and the second, among the creative writer, the readers, and the editor(s) who participate in a publication process that inevitably involves gains and losses. The questions that are asked of disciplines such as editing are trying to choose among possibilities – should one practise in this way or that? The world is big enough to have different kinds of edition from the same author, as long as the editor acknowledges that which is sacrificed by adopting one set of principles over another.

---

[56] McKenzie, *Bibliography and the Sociology of Texts*, p. 60.

[57] Ricks, 'To Criticize the Critic', p. 476.

[58] Poirier, *Poetry and Pragmatism*, p. 32.

Editors primarily create publications that encase textual scholarship. Scholarly editing is an enterprise based on what works well for the archival materials being edited. Alongside the necessary theoretical debates about the nature of texts or the standard ways to choose and emend reliable base texts, the fruit of editing 'is not *Gnosis*, but *Praxis*', to evoke Philip Sidney's comment about teaching in 'Apology for Poetrie'. Editing, as praxis, means an action-oriented application of learned principles so as to present reliable versions of works that teach others about the value of words.

2 The Author

2.1 Varieties of Intentional Experience

It is compelling that we are attracted to and have strong intuitions about authorial intention. After Andrew Crooke published an unauthorised text of one (now lost) manuscript of Thomas Browne's *Religio Medici* in 1642, Browne's defensive preface to the reader in his *authorised* edition of the following year suggests that readers

> will easily discerne the intention was not publik: and being a private exercise directed to my selfe ... It was penned in such a place and with such disadvantage, that (I protest) from the first setting of pen unto paper, I had not the assistance of any good booke, whereby to promote my invention or relieve my memory; and therefore there might be many reall lapses therein, which others might take notice of, and more than I suspected my selfe.[59]

In the following year, John Milton published his view of unconstrained authorship in *Areopagitica* (1644), which came with a conviction that 'Books are not absolutely dead things, but doe contain a potencie of life in them to be as active as that soule was whose progeny they are; nay they do preserve as in a violl the purest efficacie and extraction of that living intellect that bred them'.[60] In an environment of pre-publication censorship, the work of the elite intellect would be violated. Various forms of intend/ intention appear several times in Milton's essay, and he made the decision to print his name in grandiose type, larger than 'England', on the title page (he

[59] Browne, 'To the Reader', in *Religio Medici*. Manuscript copies of the anonymously authored *Religio Medici* had been circulating for years before Crooke's edition. Both unauthorised editions that appeared in 1642 were faithful to one of several circulating versions of Browne's manuscript, so they contain several kinds of variants.

[60] Milton, 'Areopagitica (1644)', p. 999.

also omitted the printer's name).[61] Regardless of the debates about Milton's elitism and ambivalence towards censorship, he argues that an author's intentions should not be obstructed before publication.

The examples of Browne and Milton show that authorial intentions have long been central to the published writer, but they are also mediated by social norms. Intentions need to be considered in their contexts of production and consumption. Recall Gwendolyn Brooks's encouragement to 'prevail across the editors of the world': if editors minimise authorial intention, they may also be opening themselves up to the possibility of ignoring injustices and other historical realities of authorship. As one of the primary activities of scholarly editing is to understand the author's intentions during the preparation of an accurate text, the inventions of texts are critical and creative phenomena of experience that must contend with intentionality. My goal is to elucidate a pragmatic understanding of intentionality, enacted in digital editions, that facilitates an aesthetic experience based in composition and literary experimentation. Notions of the literary writer's intentions are based on a system of linguistic and social norms that exist within triadic interactions among writers, texts, and readers. They are manifestations of agreements about how literature and authorship work in the world, and how those notions interrelate within complex networks ranging from ordinary language to legal and financial arrangements. Despite these persistent norms, academic fields have struggled to achieve a consistent understanding of this difficult concept.

Why do legal theorists and art critics take intention seriously while many literary critics dismiss it? Many artists tend to see their creations as inscrutable, but writers such as Milton and Blake desired full control over the dissemination of those mysterious things. Mark Rothko may have been unaware of what he intended in his abstract paintings, but that did not stop him from visiting the Museum of Modern Art several times a day to change the lighting to present his pictures in what he intended to be the right way

---

[61] The title page image is available at the British Library digital collection (Shelfmark G.608), www.bl.uk/collection-items/areopagitica-by-john-milton -1644.

during his solo exhibition there in 1961.[62] In one Sunday afternoon stroll through Tate Modern, I found numerous examples of clear artistic intentions. Jenny Holzer's *Protect Protect* and *Phase 1* (2007) are effective and affective because they are intentional copies of US military documents preparing for the second Iraq War – the anti-war meaning is clearly communicated. Joseph Beuys's *Was ist Kunst?* and *Jeder Mensch oder Künstler?* show how faithful copies of primary documents around a frame create another frame of artistic force, and that frame is the intentional relation which makes it an artwork. Beuys's *Was kann ich tun?* (1972) is a framed newspaper article about himself. He can do whatever he intends to do; the framing is everything.

Yet many artists emphasise the inscrutability of their art. When Huw Wheldon asked Henry Moore, in a 1960 interview with the BBC, why he created more female than male sculptures, he responded: 'That what's I'm interested in. But why – I don't know and I don't think I want to know'. Relating to artistic intention is a worry about corruption – the corruption of the artist's original intentions. Yet destruction can also be creative. Rodin believed in the life cycles of art, even campaigning against the restoration of the Parthenon after the 1894 earthquake. Hans Arp often destroyed and refashioned his paintings and sculptures, even after they had appeared in exhibitions. Gustav Metzger's auto-destructive art illustrates a conception of intention that accounts for the experiences of artists as they create and disseminate – and attempt to control the legacies of – their work, even when that means embracing decay. In his indispensable study of decay and art, Paul Taylor contrasts the view of art historians who regularly face 'corrupt' paintings with literary historians who sometimes deal with 'corrupt' texts, often with uneasiness.[63] His distinction suggests that literary scholars either take textual corruption for granted or attempt to resist the inevitable processes of change in the life of a text.

Corruption can be an aesthetic property. The artist Cai Guo-Qiang's process is to paint a picture with traditional media, and then to explode it with gunpowder.[64] What can we say about his intentions as reflected in the

---

[62] Waldman (ed.), *Mark Rothko in New York*, p. 29. [63] Taylor, *Condition*, p. 239.

[64] Guo-Qiang's 'explosion event' process was featured on episode 9 of BBC Two's *Civilisations* programme (2018).

creation of the art object, and the subsequent explosion of it? There is no necessary connection, on the one hand, between 'intention' in the artist's desire to do something with a combination of his imagination and some natural tool or technology (an inflated one in this case) and, on the other hand, 'intention' as he expected the finished artwork to mean. Cai's exploded art object is not accidental and we can infer that it is intended, but it is up to critics to say what it means, and the artist's stated meaning is no more valid than our interpretations. Intentions and aesthetic properties are embodied in Cai's work, which combines the actions of the artist and the natural accidents in the bringing of the work into being. Intention in art is like the lighting of the firework, but where that firework goes and what it will do are unpredictable. According to Cai's Taoist framework, the artwork is a process of interacting with nature, and building a bridge between the imagination and the natural world – an apt metaphor for the act of writing.

Acts of creation, and authorial intentions, are fluid. Percy Shelley also saw intention as one thing and his execution of it as another matter: 'when composition begins, inspiration is already on the decline, and the most glorious poetry that has ever been communicated to the world is probably a feeble shadow of the original conceptions of the poet'.[65] That struggle for 'verbal consciousness', which is never realised, also appears in D. H. Lawrence's foreword to *Women in Love*, in which the writer attempts 'to understand what is happening, even in himself, as he goes along,' not as 'a superimposition of a theory' but rather as a 'passionate struggle into conscious being'. Shelley and Lawrence are both evoking the romantic notion of the ungraspability of idea and feeling as well as the inadequacy of language to capture feeling. Yet Lawrence disputes the goal of theorising his experience of his own creativity into singular generalisations.

Robert Graves echoed these ideas by saying that, in writing poetry, 'a sort of cloud descends on you', and

> you suddenly realise there is some problem of extreme
> importance that's got to be solved. And then you realise

---

[65] In his *Critique of Modern Textual Criticism*, pp. 102–3, McGann cites this quote to undermine authorial intention in favour of 'institutional conditions'.

> there's a poem around ... It's as though the poem has
> already been written but you're trying to reconstitute
> it ... So you work hard and hard to finally get it back to
> something near what it really is, was, or would be.[66]

Graves emphasised that writing is experiential and contingent, even 'mystical'.

Elaborating on an epigraph by Kafka in his 1949 novel *The Sheltering Sky* ('From a certain point onward there is no longer any turning back; that is the point that must be reached'), the great literary craftsman Paul Bowles said about his writing process:

> ... when I got to that point, beyond which there was no
> turning back, I decided to use a surrealist technique – simply
> writing without any thought of what I had already written,
> or awareness of what I was writing, or intention as to what
> I was going to write next, or how it was going to finish. And
> I did that.[67]

He decided to act, and that decision was to not think *about* where the writing was going. Bowles distinguishes intention in action as against beliefs, self-consciousness, or future wishes – that is, where the text happens to be going. Although the fleeting thoughts and feelings of the author might be lost, the object of editorial attention, the thoughts inscribed in the text (the *aboutness* of the language) cannot be escaped. But there is no author in control of his thoughts; there are only processes and relationships – composition.

These random forays into the visual and literary arts undermine Tanselle's view that the goal of editing is to reconstruct, 'as accurately as possible, the text finally intended by the author'.[68] Instead, the editor may embrace Wimsatt and Beardsley's view of the 'intentional fallacy' – namely,

[66] Interview with Malcolm Muggeridge, BBC, 1965.

[67] Bowles, *Conversations with Paul Bowles*, p. 88.

[68] Tanselle, 'The Varieties of Scholarly Editing', in Greetham (ed.), *Scholarly Editing*, p. 16.

that interpretations of a text cannot be based on assumptions about the author's intended meaning and other biographical information.[69] The work, as a well-wrought urn, takes on a life of its own, so authorial intentions can be no basis for critical judgements. This is a valid position that has led decades of critics to conclude that there is little value in studying intentions – culminating in Roland Barthes' 'The Death of the Author' (1967), which contends that authors and their intentions cease to exist after their work is released to readers. But this is a mistaken view for textual editing because Wimsatt and Beardsley were attempting to control and isolate the concept of literary meaning by only generating analyses from the deracinated form of the finished text alone. John Bryant has shown that intention is a constraint for both critical and social text editing, articulating an Intentional Fallacy Fallacy that static notions of agency and temporality cannot represent a creative process: 'To isolate these modalities in a given time period is to compartmentalize authorial intention, and make an abstraction out of the concrete realities of creation'.[70]

These attempts at literary meaning are probabilistic, but still worth attending to; any 'certainty' of texts has never been available, as Sir Thomas Browne himself showed, but that cannot mean suspending any attempts to understand the meanings communicated by literary artists. A full investigation of the text, let alone a deep appreciation of the work, requires an understanding of context – ranging from the author's actions and life circumstances to questions of publication processes. That there is a difference between intention vis-à-vis the creative process and the author's wishes or desires before and after composition means that we should be even more attentive to the varieties of intentionality, and seek to determine which kinds of intention are at play in archives and editions, whether in working draft manuscripts recording a private creative process or in post-publication mediations of texts in an institutional realm. Intentions matter, but they may not always be what you think they are.

Attending to *intentional relations* reveals the exchanges among writers, raw materials (texts), and readers in a literary circuit within a 'complex

[69] Wimsatt and Beardsley, 'The Intentional Fallacy', p. 469.

[70] Bryant, *The Fluid Text*, pp. 8–9, 42.

cultural background'.[71] The textual critic could then look to Emerson, who wrote that 'poems are a corrupt version of some text in nature with which they ought to be made to tally'.[72] *Made to tally*: this phrase implies the presence of readers transcending from poem to nature, to 'participate' in 'the invention of nature' with imagination and intellect, 'sharing the path or *circuit* of things through forms, and so making them *translucid to others*'.[73] Emerson wants writing to tally with nature (Me and Not Me), but I would like to push Emerson's tallying further to include the reader in his 'circuit'. He implies as much with his invitation for us to 'participate in the invention of nature', but if poems come out of nature, then they are a common inheritance accessible to all. Whitman invoked Emerson's tallying in several poems – for example, 'Passing the song of the hermit bird and the tallying song of my / soul' in his elegy to Lincoln, 'When Lilacs Last in the Dooryard Bloom'd'.[74] For Emerson and Whitman sensed that in 'nature' writers and readers meet each other halfway, with neither asserting their supremacy – Poirier called it 'a struggle between what you want to make of a text and what it wants to make of itself and of you'.[75] A text never gives readers the 'precise sense of the author', but readers can and should be able to access the manipulations of words that the writer meant to tally with their initial inspiration. Emersonian tallying entails a proper respect for writers' and readers' intentions as well as forms of experimentation and craft, and an attempt to tally both. Emerson's apt word 'tally' means not only calculating and reckoning (a form of computation and analysis) but also narrating. Past works of literature are made useful to the present when editors prepare and tally those creative works with current technologies and analytical methods.

---

[71] See Lamarque, *Work and Object*, pp. 19, 40–1, 67–9. The 'complex cultural background' includes a range of contexts from conventions to politics and technologies.

[72] Emerson, 'The Poet', in Cramer (ed.), *The Portable Emerson*, p. 248.

[73] Ibid., p. 249; my emphases.

[74] Whitman, *Leaves of Grass*, p. 262. Accessed at the Walt Whitman Archive, https://whitmanarchive.org/published/LG/1891/poems/193.

[75] Poirier, *Poetry and Pragmatism*, p. 167.

Intention is derived from the Latin *intentio* ('directed at'), which shows its essential connection to thought, language, and action. Language requires actors, and language must be about something. As the pre-Socratic philosopher Parmenides is reported to have argued, every thought is *of* something; if it were any other way, then language would be referring to nothing.[76] A full account of authorial intention would take up an entire book and test many readers' patience. One important takeaway concerns a philosophical distinction between actions and beliefs: language requires intentions, but beliefs about the meaning of language are not the same as the intentions that generated them. Following Wittgenstein's aphorism, 'For a *large* class of cases – though not for all . . . the meaning of a word is its use in the language',[77] Anscombe formulated three kinds of intentionality: *intentional action* (acting intentionally), *intention with which* (acting with the intention or awareness of doing something), and an *expression of intention for the future* (beliefs and desires).[78] Some textual scholars have gravitated towards John Searle's modification of Anscombe's theory that proposes that intentionality is a property of several mental states, akin to speech acts, that accounts for the way the mind is directed at, or about, objects or states of affairs. Whereas intentionality refers to directedness, intentions are just one kind of intentionality among many others, including beliefs, desires, hopes, and fears.[79] Writing is a deliberate act of meaning-making.[80]

[76] See Plato's *Parmenides*, 132b–c.

[77] Wittgenstein, *Philosophical Investigations*, p. 20e, section 43.

[78] On theories of intentionality, see Brentano, *Psychology from an Empirical Standpoint*; Anscombe, *Intention*. In textual criticism, see Hancher, 'Three Kinds of Intention'; Tanselle, 'The Editorial Problem of Final Authorial Intention'; Bushell, *Text as Process*.

[79] Searle, *Intentionality*, pp. 1–3.

[80] Ibid., pp. 8–9. Searle also argued in his debate with Derrida that in both speaking and writing, 'there is no getting away from intentionality, because a *meaningful sentence is just a standing possibility of the corresponding intentional speech act*. To understand it, it is necessary to know that anyone who said it and meant it would be performing that speech act determined by the rules of the languages that give the sentence its meaning in the first place' ('Reiterating the Differences', p. 202).

Writers must have intentions, and reasons for their corresponding actions, but they are best understood through actions and practices (*experience*) rather than psychology. Beliefs about those texts are not the same as the intentions that created them. For the editor, then, the actions and practices of writers are the most useful anchors of decision-making. The Anscombe-Searle view is narrow in the sense of being an *internalist* account that focuses on the individual's direct perceptions ('mental states') of speech acts; the danger in such an approach is that it uses a doubleness (e.g., mind and object) to understand an essentially triadic phenomenon of speakers, utterances, and interpreters in particular situations. As Hilary Putnam argued, mental states and utterances are understood not by their internal physical structure alone but by their varying *external* functions in the world – the causal relations between speakers in communities and their environment.[81]

If speech is 'nothing but signs of direction in thought', as William James argued, then language produces signs reflecting 'psychic transitions'. James may have been thinking of Emerson's pithy statement that 'Words are also actions, and actions are a kind of words'.[82] When an author begins to write, 'the real work has been previously done', and the activity entails a 'sensible report to direct his completion of the work' that is to be delivered to 'the common world', as Dewey put it.[83] The 'sensible report to direct' a completion of the work reinforces the importance of intention as directedness, while the experience of that work enters the 'common world'. The editor must attempt to account for both to make texts more fulfilling and meaningful.

Dewey added that language is 'held together by a sincere emotion that controls the material', and that sincerity is an intentional notion that 'calls attention to structural properties discernible in the work itself'.[84] This sincerity may be an inheritance from Romanticism, but he was gesturing

---

[81] Putnam, 'Philosophy and Our Mental Life', pp. 291–303. See also Soames, 'Analytic Philosophy of Language', and Dewey, *Art as Experience*, p. 295.

[82] Emerson, 'The Poet', in Cramer (ed.), *The Portable Emerson*, p. 240.

[83] Dewey, *Art as Experience*, pp. 25–26, 53.

[84] Manns, 'Intentionalism in John Dewey's Aesthetics', p. 418.

to the importance of the artist's attempt to convey messages to an audience in their work. If the literary work is an attempt at communication, then the writer's intention must be carried forward in a meaningful way to a 'community of experience'.[85] Literature provides insight into the nature of intentions, and the reciprocal nature of intentionality – for there is an intentionality in literary appreciation, too.[86] When both sides of this enigmatic communication of thoughts are working out, the subject moves beyond ordinary experience and towards aesthetic experience. The problem, which Emerson knew well, is that literature relies on indirection – or 'being in indirection', as Robert Frost put it in his lecture 'On Education'.

The reality is, we interpret language on the hoof, as Donald Davidson articulated with his 'passing theory' of communication and interpretation. Language comes with an intention that an audience will grasp intended meanings and ulterior purpose(s).[87] If intentions are connected to expectations that words will lead to a certain outcome, then a writer must have some beliefs that the audience will interpret those words as they were intended – Davidson calls this 'interpretive charity'. 'The writer', says Davidson, 'cannot ignore what his readers know or assume about the words he uses, and such knowledge and expectations can only come from the reader's exposure to past usage'.[88] That sounds like the standard intentionalist view. However, as Davidson puts it elsewhere,

> the interpreter comes to the occasion of utterance armed with a theory that tells him (or so he believes) what an arbitrary utterance of the speaker means. The speaker then

---

[85] Manns, 'Intentionalism in John Dewey's Aesthetics', p. 420; Davidson, *Truth, Language, and History*, pp. 180–1.

[86] See Dewey, *Art as Experience*, pp. 50–4.

[87] See also the 'Gricean Reflex' of 'implicature' in Grice, *Studies in the Way of Words*.

[88] Davidson, 'James Joyce and Humpty Dumpty', in *Truth, Language, and History*, p. 147. See also Rorty, 'The Contingency of Language', in *Contingency, Irony, and Solidarity*, pp. 14–15. My thanks to Barry C. Smith for suggesting these readings.

says something with the intention that it will be interpreted in a certain way, and the expectation that it will be so interpreted ... But the speaker is nevertheless understood; the interpreter adjusts his theory so that it yields the speaker's intended interpretation.[89]

Davidson uses malapropisms as a thought experiment showing why passing theories are needed to adjust our understanding of what a given malapropism means, but this situation is also applicable to the ways in which we come to understand analogies, ironies, and other forms of literary language. We bring to each experience of a text a set of 'prior theories' – assumptions, knowledge, beliefs, associations (or what psychologists call 'implicit' memories) – or a set of educated guesses about what to do to understand words under different conditions. The passing theory is an adjustment in action based on an understanding of available evidence, whereas the 'prior theory' is the set of beliefs and expectations prior to the exchange. As Davidson puts it, a passing theory is always subject to correction and it improves as the 'evidential base enlarges': 'the prior theory expresses how he is prepared in advance to interpret an utterance of the speaker, while the passing theory is how he *does* interpret the utterance ... [and] is the theory he *intends* the interpreter to use'.[90] Passing theories of communication are successful insofar as they have satisfied a demand for description and adequate interpretation of intentions – facilitating us 'to construct a correct, that is, convergent, passing theory for speech transactions'.[91] Agreement is reached when prior theories become more and more alike.

Theories are 'passing' because they are not only *passing between* people but also *passing the test* of explanation, recalling William James's analogy that truth resides on a 'credit system': 'Our thoughts and beliefs "pass," so long as nothing challenges them'.[92] Passing theories either can refine prior theories for future use or can be discarded when they are no longer useful.

[89] Davidson, 'A Nice Derangement of Epitaphs', in *Essential Davidson*, p. 258.

[90] Ibid., pp. 260–1. [91] Ibid., p. 264.

[92] James, 'Pragmatism's Conception of Truth', in McDermott (ed.), *The Writings of William James*, p. 433.

Davidson's argument resonates with the way that scholars gauge the implied and direct messages communicated to them by archival documents, and how theories are adjusted based on an activity of 'passing' between (or meeting) the evidence of the intentions, entering new hypotheses, and revising past interpretations. Literature, as principled rhetoric, requires two or more participants.[93] Literature is also 'a report on experience', as Louis Menand put it.[94] Writing comes with the desire to say something meaningful, and to be heard. Accounting for both the writer's intentions to principled rhetoric as well as the experiences of rhetoric itself, the passing theory illustrates the importance of original intentions while claiming the importance of exchanges through mediation.

Davidson models these exchanges as 'intersubjective triangulation' – the writer, audience, and a 'common background' – which locates the common stimulus in literary materials.[95] Literature *invites* meaning in some direction (*intentio*, again) – yet, as Victor Kestenbaum argues, '[t]he poet's and writer's struggles, their possibilizing in language, ought not, and probably will not, establish comforting equivalences between the poem's or story's meanings and my meanings'.[96] Applying the intersubjective triangulation model into editing entails an exchange modelled not on a one-to-one correspondence between texts and readers' meanings but on the reciprocal effects of documentary traces of thought on interpreters, and the reactions of interpreters, and the constructive events of communication itself, as Susan Greenberg has also argued.[97] Umberto Eco distinguishes among

---

[93] On 'principled rhetoric', see Ricks, 'Literature as Against Theory', in *Essays in Appreciation*, pp. 311–12. On rhetoric-as-exchange, see Aristotle's *Rhetoric* I.1 1354a1, and I.2 1355b26f and 1356a25f.

[94] Menand, 'Afterword, 2007', in Menand, *Discovering Modernism*, p. 165.

[95] Davidson, 'Locating Literary Language', in *Truth, Language, and History*, p. 177. Davidson's view relates to Peirce's three categories of experience, namely that experience comes out of the triadic nexus of memories/ideas, perceptions, and mediation/intentions. See Bernstein, *The Pragmatic Turn*, pp. 132–4.

[96] Kestenbaum, *The Grace and Severity of the Ideal*, pp. 62–3.

[97] Greenberg, *A Poetics of Editing*, pp. 62–5, also discusses Davidson's triangulation model, but my aim is to extend the idea of passing theories to practices in intentionality and digital media.

the intentions of the author, the reader, and the text, and argues that the text – *intentio operis*, a 'machine' – is the meeting point between author and reader. Yet Eco's machine is itself a multifaceted thing, consisting of layers of verbal and non-verbal material features. Eco seeks to both activate and constrain the reader using a Popperian falsification principle of textual intentions; whether intentions are hypothetical or actual is another matter that goes beyond my scope.[98] A textual condition in flux calls for passing theories of intention – for they are subject to consensus as well as the possibility that more temporal information will arise in the network.

Discussions of intentionality in textual editing tend to make a strong claim for the author's intentions (and undermine the reader) or undermine authorial intention and privilege the reader's response or abstract stories about social forces of publishing. Both sides of the debate neglect the role of the experience of interpreting and meaning-making. Dewey's idea of 'funded' experience and 'reconstructive doing' gives value to prior theories that account for individuals' deep encounters with texts. These experiences are fundamentally rooted in intentional exchanges, as well as a 'balance between doing and receiving'.[99] Even writers, as their own first readers, have passing theories of their own writing. When a person examines a manuscript in an archive or reads a book, they are experiencing an exchange of meaning-making with the author's inscribed and mediated thoughts. But seeing a manuscript with revisions is not enough; experience does not end there; readers must situate those inscriptions within additional contexts, such as stories about the author's publishing process or peripheral evidence in the archive or biographical information. The passing theory stipulates that readers' responses matter *because* they are engaging with the making of writers' texts, which by their nature do have intended meanings that need to be tallied, even if

---

[98] For more on hypothetical and actual intentionalism, see Carroll, 'Interpretation and Intention' and Maes, 'Intention, Interpretation, and Contemporary Visual Art'.

[99] Dewey, *Art as Experience*, p. 47. See also p. 56: 'a beholder must *create* his own experience. And his creation must include relations comparable to those which the original producer underwent'.

imperfectly. Writers' intentions therefore matter, but so too do the theories that interpreters bring to the subject matter.

Editorial decisions must also contend with social processes, but minimising intention would still be unwise with authors such as Mark Twain, who changed his intentions based on social expectations in some instances, but in other contexts provided explicit instructions to his publishers not to change aspects of his writing, such as his spelling and punctuation. There are several entertaining examples, but, to illustrate the point, here is the opening to one of his letters to his publisher while he was preparing *The Innocents Abroad* in 1869:

> A proof-reader who persists in making two words ˄(& sometimes even compound words)˄ of "anywhere" and "everything;" & who spells villainy "villiany" & "liquifies" &c, &c, is ~~not three removes from an idiot.~~ ˄infernally unreliable – ˄ & so I don't like to trust your man. He never yet has acceded to a request of mine made in the margin, in the matter of spelling & punctuation, as I know of. He shows spite – don't trust him, but revise my revises yourself. I have long ago given up trying to get him to spell those first-mentioned words properly.[100]

As McGann says, the 'structure of agreements' between parties forms the locus of textual transmission, and 'literary works are not produced without arrangements of some sort'.[101] Yet the 'structure of agreements' between Mark Twain and his publishers would sometimes break down. Correcting those breakdowns is a luxury that scholarly editors have which is not always available to the publishing processes Twain was dealing with in 1869, when he was at once revising previously published newspaper pieces and composing

---

[100] Mark Twain, 20 April 1869 letter to Elisha Bliss, accessed at the *Mark Twain Project Online*, www.marktwainproject.org/xtf/view?docId=letters/UCCL00286.xml; searchAll=;sectionType1=;sectionType2=;sectionType3=;sectionType4=; sectionType5=;style=letter;brand=mtp#1.

[101] McGann, *A Critique of Modern Textual Criticism*, p. 48.

fresh new copy from memory in haste to pad the book.[102] The important point is which authorial processes and practices are worth privileging.

Writers and readers must *conceive* of the text as literature for it to be accepted as such by others.[103] We may have different interpretations that are made to tally with the work, but readers still experience one work, even when encountering many texts of a work, and theories of intention need to be anchored to the writer's documented actions and histories.[104] Documents like Twain's above carry important intentions that scholars can and should take time to interpret and judge as to their value, but the interpretations do affect the meanings of texts. Passing theories also account for the inevitable discrepancies that occasion textual editing.

The following passage from the opening of Melville's *Billy Budd*, for example, has at least two anomalies in manuscript:

> Some of 'em do his washing, darn his old trowzers for him; the carpenter is at odd times making a pretty little chest of drawers for him. Anybody will do any thing for Billy Budd; and it's the happy family here. But now, Lieutenant, if that young fellow goes – I know how it will be aboard the "Rights." Not again very soon, shall I, coming up from dinner, lean over the capstain smoking a quiet pipe – no, not very soon again, I think.

I think 'trowzers' and 'capstain' are oddities. I adjust by looking up 'trowzers' in the *OED* and realising that it was an acceptable spelling of

---

[102] See Hirst, 'The Making of *The Innocents Abroad*: 1867–1872'.

[103] Lamarque, *Work and Object*, pp. 40 and 68. See also his 'Wittgenstein, Literature, and the Idea of a Practice', pp. 380–1: 'to establish that the concept of literature is modern would require showing that there has been a radical break between our modern practice of engaging with literary works and earlier practices, involving judgements, evaluations, and interests, encompassing poetry and drama. The evidence suggests there has been no such break'.

[104] Dasenbrock, 'Do We Write the Text We Read?', in Dasenbrock (ed.), *Literary Theory after Davidson*, pp. 24–5.

'trousers' in Melville's time; 'capstain' is still strange, but it is also an archaic spelling that was in use in the eighteenth century. But Melville first wrote 'capstan', the 'correct' spelling, and in a later revision, he altered 'capstan' to 'capstain'. This revision not only underscores Melville's close attention to the nautical language of the period but also reflects the dialect of his character in this chapter, Captain Graveling, an eighteenth-century mariner. Given all of these adjustments to my prior theory of Melville the poor speller, I leave Melville's archaic spellings as-is (that is what he wrote, after all). What matters to me is not 'correcting' the NN editors; rather, it is understanding the practices of composition and publication that editors have employed in the past, and how those theories can be made to tally with new critical possibilities.

The design of the standard editor's textual apparatus further demonstrates a missed opportunity for elucidating passing theories. The 'capstain' variant in Melville could be recorded in a critical apparatus note:

capstan] capstain (MS)

This note does not indicate *why* or *how* the MS was modified; nor are the modifications seen. In some instances, editors could elucidate their rationale in a separate section of textual notes, but that is yet another example of a limited use of technology (of the book). A functional concept of intentionality carries over nicely into digital editing. In the MEL digital edition, we encoded the manuscript in TEI XML:

```
<del rend="_ink1" hand="#HM" change="StBb"
   facs="#img_51-0044">capstan</del>
<add place="inline" rend="no-caret _ink1"
   hand="#HM" change="StBb" facs="#img_51-
   0044">capstain</add>
```

This is an interpretive activity of meaning-making – using semantic deletion and addition tags to explicate the acts of substitution and link to a page image – which improves upon the original apparatus entry. Tagging is a form of naming a phenomenon in the text – and this naming by the editor constitutes a form of *attention*, a kind of intention informed by the editor's passing theory of the author's intentions. MEL explains the textual crux in a revision narrative that is accessible as a note in the reading text. In 1996, David Greetham reported that scholars rarely cite information from the textual apparatus of scholarly editions they are using.[105] I fear this is still true today. How can digital editors guide readers to the evidence in textual apparatus better than their print predecessors? Again, usefulness matters. Davidson's model of interpretation suggests that editors ought to refine theories based on experience, adjusting them based on difference, and explicating their functions through semantic data and transparent narratives and interfaces – these are modes of attention grounded in composition and experimentation.

Several distinguished textual scholars have attempted to analyse the problem of intentionality through the creative process, showing that the matter of authorial intention can be neither decontextualised nor depersonalised.[106] Despite the tension between the writer's intentions and meanings, it is more productive to understand and embrace the source of the tension by acknowledging 'the power of innovation and creativity in the use of language', as Davidson suggests.[107] The anti-intentionalist is (probably unintentionally) closing themselves off to questions of creativity – and creative interpretations of creativity. Editors still need to be able to consult intention or relevant data to understand the textual situation. What we mean by intention involves both causal and formal relations to the objects of editing, which are the inscribed words.

Authorial intention, social processes of editing, and reader response are feedback loops of experience. A writer expresses what they mean in a circuit of perceiving, acting, evaluating the consequences of acts of inscription, and integrating what they learned into new acts of writing. Then the editor works through the same process by encountering the author, and so goes

---

[105] Greetham, 'Textual Forensics', pp. 41–2.

[106] See Bryant, *The Fluid Text*, pp. 10–11; Bushell, *Text as Process*, pp. 32 and 219; Parker, *Flawed Texts and Verbal Icons*, p. 22; Thorpe, *Principles of Textual Criticism*, p. 38.

[107] Davidson, 'James Joyce and Humpty Dumpty', in *Truth, Language, and History*, p. 143.

the reader. Experience is *experimental*, a process of development and discovery by writers and readers.[108] To study authorial intentions is to examine the basis of such experimentation, *composition* – which Dewey would say opens up 'new fields of experience'.

An account of intentionality succeeds when the prior theories originating in the documentary evidence agree with the passing theories of editors and readers that are attending to the material. They depend on each other's mutual coherence to be meaningful. Such a reciprocity opens up editing in the digital space, constituting a future-focused, fluid form of textual scholarship, as against a backward-looking, teleological one. The textual situation is the product of contingencies – redescriptions of texts, rather than new insights into the nature of texts (or social forces or readers). What Dewey called 'doings and undergoings' are activities that connect the productive and appreciative aspects of art.[109] The contingency of literary history means that editors will invent texts by creating new metaphors for new prior theories, not as a demonstration of the nature of texts and works, or of retrieving true meanings of intentions, but as 'better tools' for working with, and reflecting on, texts.[110] These interpretations can now be documented in the data.

2.2 *Exhibition 1: Herman Melville's* Billy Budd, Sailor *(c. 1886– 1891)*

Using digital approaches to convey passing theories of intentionality enhances the editing of Herman Melville's *Billy Budd*, *Sailor*, an unfinished work that survives in a complicated manuscript. A digital edition of such a work, by attending to what Richard Poirier saw as the connection between experience and composition, attempts to illuminate the principle that 'life may be created out of words'.[111] Editing *Billy Budd* for MEL helped me to understand Melville's writing process in new ways. What I had read and thought before, and what I thought I had understood, could not match the unfolding lexical

---

[108] Grimstad, *Experience and Experimental Writing*, pp. 12–14.

[109] Dewey, *Art as Experience*, p. 23 and *passim*.

[110] Rorty, 'The Contingency of Language', in *Contingency, Irony, and Solidarity*, p. 21.

[111] Poirier, 'Why Do Pragmatists Want to Be Like Poets?', p. 353.

patterns, and the visualisations of the stages of revision that suggest a new kind of code – Melville's experimentation with form. A language within a language, the computations of Melville's text are fluid, not fixed.

Billy Budd was rushed into publication as part of the Melville revival in the 1920s to complete the Constable edition of the author's works. Thus began the canonisation of *Billy Budd*, a halted text-in-progress that occasioned flawed editions beginning with Raymond Weaver's Constable edition in 1924 and followed by F. Barron Freeman's 1948 Harvard University Press edition. They were flawed because they gave the wrong impression of a finished text, which perhaps is best evidenced by the decision to print a discarded section from the middle of the story as the preface because Elizabeth Melville inscribed in pencil 'Preface?' at the beginning of the group of discarded leaves. *Billy Budd* came before the public as a finished work for decades before Merton Sealts, Jr and Harrison Hayford published their extraordinary study of the manuscript in the 1962 University of Chicago Press genetic edition. The resulting situation is a canonical but incomplete text with an unfounded historical mandate in place for a clean copy of Melville's 'final masterpiece'. Building on Sealts and Hayford's work, the 2017 NN edition published a new, critical, unmodernised text of *Billy Budd*. The NN edition is an admirable improvement on the already admirable Hayford-Sealts edition, which regularised aspects of Melville's punctuation and phraseology, in that it attempted to preserve the rough quality (the odd punctuation and awkward phrases) of the manuscript.

As a result of the incompleteness of the manuscript, the NN adopts a policy of adhering to Melville's 'latest intentions', creating the necessity for editorial liberties. Latest intentions are distinguished from final intentions because the work was never completed. Editors judge intentions based on what was left on the unfinished manuscript pages. However, it is impossible to ascertain what Melville's final intentions might have been, considering that the best evidence for intentions is inscribed on the messy, unfinished manuscript. As I said in the previous section, if intentions have not been enacted or communicated, then they cannot be ascertained. Intentions, as future wishes, could not have been realised in this case, so the only intentions to consider as evidence are on the page. The NN edition leaves no signals in the reading text indicating where there are rough patches of unfinished revision and where there are more polished bits. Publishing a reading text is very useful, but with the digital edition at MEL a reader can access both a critical reading text as well as the textual cruxes through the highlighted in-text pop-up notes and manuscript image thumbnails linking to manuscript leaves, diplomatic transcriptions, and revision sequences.[112] An unfinished text requires even more responsiveness and transparency for the reader's experience of the edition than would be expected in a finished work. Thinking computationally and pragmatically about the material, the MEL editors of the digital edition of *Billy Budd* focus on enhancing the user's experience of the composition of this complicated text.

In principle, adhering to a latest intention works insofar as the editor thinks of the edition as an approximation of the latest inscriptions in the manuscript. However, the NN editors still struggle with the issue of 'latest' authorial intention, as if pursuing something beyond the intention in action that 'latest intention' implies. As the 'General Note on the Text' indicates, the critical edition aims 'to present Melville's intention in the act of writing – indeed, his latest intention at points where the manuscripts show his revisions of earlier intentions'.[113] The note adds that the unfinished nature of the writings means that 'it would be wrong to say that the NN texts reflect Melville's final intention for each work; they simply aim to offer his latest intentions evident in the manuscripts that have survived'. The rationale for emending latest intentions is that '[c]arrying out this aim requires making some alterations in the wording, punctuation, capitalization, and spelling of the latest text present in each document'.[114] In obvious mistakes of omission, redundancy, and (sometimes) spelling, the NN policy is reasonable. Yet in other, more difficult cases, where incomplete revisions leave syntactic gaps, alternate word choices, misplaced words, or dropped punctuation, the NN editors change what Melville had inscribed in the manuscript.

The NN decisions sometimes envisage a text that never came into being, at least not by Melville. In some instances, the 'latest intention' of an incomplete revision imposes a logic of conjectural emendation similar to

---

[112] Bryant, Kelley, and Ohge, *Versions of* Billy Budd, Sailor.

[113] Melville, *Billy Budd, Sailor*, pp. 368–9.   [114] Ibid., p. 369.

an assumed final intention in eclectic text editing, which is reinforced by language such as 'presumably' and 'presuming', 'perhaps intended', and 'might/would have' in the textual notes. In such cases, multiple options exist in the place of one word, so the editors have imagined what Melville might have changed or restored if he had lived long enough to finish the book. Melville 'often failed to carry a revision through completely, leaving a construction that is obviously incoherent and clearly unintended', so the reading text 'attempts to bring about the intended reading'.[115]

The confusion in the manuscript provides grounds for the NN editors to choose an *earlier* reading that was more complete or to print a conjectural reading that the editors prefer over the manuscript when a late revision is incomplete or vacillating among multiple, viable word options occupying the same space. The 'latest intention' policy is inconsistently applied because it sometimes restores an earlier wording that Melville attempted to revise, and perhaps inconsistency is not a bad thing given the contingencies of writing and revision. The problem with that reasoning is that the line of demarcation between intentions (and aesthetic coherence) is sometimes impossible to know. It is also suspect for any editor to claim to have the capacity to 'bring about an intended reading' when an author did not finish revising, or that the editor might be capable of making judgements about the point at which the author had revised too much and damaged the aesthetic integrity of the work.

At the end of chapter 25, for example, Melville rewrote Billy's execution scene without settling on a satisfactory ending that describes Billy's lifeless 'pinioned figure' in relation to the ship's motion. As Melville wrote in ink and later revised the final sentence in pencil, it ends with 'the slow roll of the hull, in moderate weather so majestic in a great ship ponderously-cannoned'. But Melville then bracketed 'in moderate . . . cannoned', indicated in a marginal note to move that phrase to the previous page, and ended the sentence with 'the ship's motion' instead of 'the slow roll of the hull'.[116] Afterward, he deleted the marginal note, which, according to the editors, 'presumably' signals Melville's intention to restore the bracketed phrase, but that is far from certain on the manuscript (he could have

[115] Ibid. [116] Ibid., p. 533.

intended to retain 'ship's motion' without moving the bracketed phrase; or he was unsure of what to do next). Because of the incompleteness of the revisions, the NN edition disregards Melville's late addition of 'ship's motion' and restores the wording before he bracketed the final part of the sentence – 'as Melville presumably intended doing'.[117] No print edition can offer an efficient way to tell the difference between leaves like these, with Melville's unvarnished mind on display *in medias res*, and other leaves that were earlier inked fair copies and subject to less revision.

Any completed editorial process would have included changes made by copy-editors seeking to bring Melville's draft into conformity with house style, and Hayford and Sealts, in their version of *Billy Budd*, did that work on Melville's behalf. On the other hand, Melville could have completed any of the incomplete revisions and changed his mind in any number of ways. The Hayford and Sealts edition, while being a magisterial scholarly achievement, is an invention of the text that includes more editorial interpolation than Melville's publishers would have initiated. The genetic transcription of *Billy Budd* in the editorial appendix of the NN edition, which is a minimal revision of the Hayford-Sealts transcription, is accurate but is itself relegated to the back, and difficult to read owing to the genetic symbols embedded in the transcriptions that attempt to represent modes of revision and sequencing. This decision consigns this evidence to appendices that are likely to be removed from further reprintings of *Billy Budd*.

With NN's reading text, readers have no way of knowing these problems, unless, after some frustration with navigating between the reading text and the textual apparatus in the back of the book, the reader absorbs the textual notes and the genetic transcriptions. Readers may then have a closer experience with Melville's creative process, but the textual apparatus makes it hard to gain a clear sense of the textual problem from this NN edition, and the edition does not reproduce the manuscript leaves for visual inspection. The digital approach is much easier: MEL has its own rough approximation of Melville's final text (called a base text), but the difficulties and the emendations are highlighted for the reader, as is the original manuscript. The transcriptions of the manuscripts in MEL are encoded in XML

---

[117] Ibid., pp. 65, 431.

according to the standards of the Text Encoding Initiative (http://tei-c.org/) using the TextLab editing tool, which matches facsimile zones to the bits of relevant transcriptions: revision sites and other metamarks (e.g., folio marks).

The NN edition meddles in ways that would adversely affect a computational analysis of the text. For example, in a description of Billy in chapter 1, the editors changed Melville's 'he' to 'handsome sailor'.[118] The 'he' in that sentence is emended to 'handsome sailor' in the NN edition because the phrase is an 'incomplete revision' that 'would presumably have been rectified by Melville'.[119] Hayford left 'he' alone in his University of Chicago reading text because the referent was clear enough in context. Any text analyst who was intrigued by a certain number of instances of 'he' or 'handsome sailor' – a crucial term Melville develops in the novella – would find one more instance of the phrase than Melville wrote. Users of the edition will not be consulting the correct frequency of Melville's usage but how many times the NN editors thought he meant to write it.

In some other cases, editorial overreaches or meddling in a previous edition would influence and carry over into the next edition. For example, in an important section of chapter 3, Melville compares the Great Mutiny (at Spithead and Nore, 1797) to the aftermath of the French Revolution. The diplomatic transcription in Figure 2 shows that Melville alluded to the irony of 'the devotion of the British tar, to the throne, that is, to the state, to his country'. He then added 'patriotic' before 'devotion', and deleted 'to the throne, that is, to the state, to his country: –'. He then restored those lines but decided to delete (again) 'to the state'. Melville restored parts of the deletion, so the final wording should be:

> the patriotic devotion of the British tar, that is, to his country: –
> "*And as for my life, t'is the King's!*"

Hayford and Sealts transcribed it this way in their genetic transcription in the back of their edition, but for some reason they dropped 'that is, to his

---

[118] Ibid., pp. 3–4, 443. [119] Ibid., p. 410.

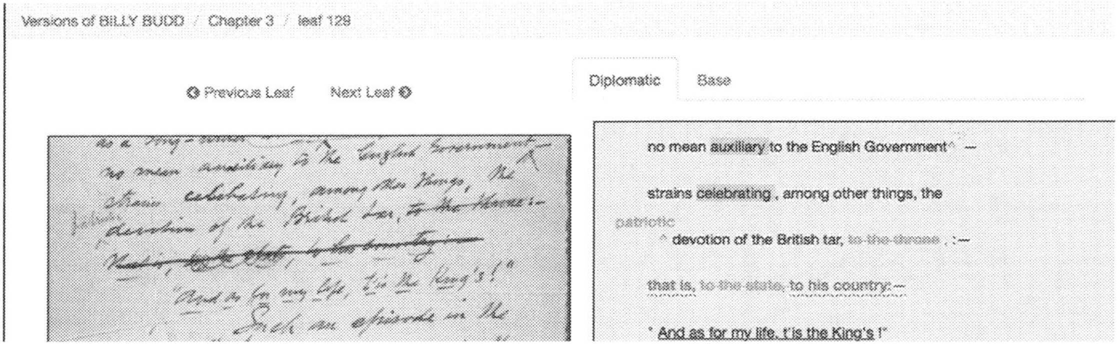

Figure 2 Manuscript transcription from *Billy Budd*, ch. 3 (MEL, https://app.textlab.org/transcriptions/15517).

country: – ' from their reading text. Hayford and Sealts did not explain their reasoning, but the NN followed suit and included a note arguing that this was yet another instance of an incomplete revision because Melville neglected to resolve the redundancy in 'patriotic' and 'to his country'. That logic betrays Melville's pencilled addition of the word 'patriotic' in the same sequence of restoring 'that is, to his country'. The phrase is not redundant, for a British subject can have a patriotic devotion to his country (e.g., Scotland) whilst being ambivalent about his state (the United Kingdom, containing several countries). It is not known whether Melville was thinking along these lines, but the NN critical text forecloses the possibilities of analysing the nuances of British patriotism in Melville's uncompleted revision.

With a text such as *Billy Budd*, the editor will need to make decisions to clean up the prose for the sake of coherence, but sometimes that desire for consistency betrays Melville's intentions. Consider the seeming inconsistency at the end of chapter 13, in which the narrator describes a 'peculiar conscience assigned to be the private mentor of Claggart. And, for the rest, not improbably it put him upon new experiments'. That is, this is how the MEL text renders these two sentences. The NN text reads: 'peculiar conscience assigned to be the private mentor of Claggart; and, for the rest, not improbably it put him upon new experiments'. This difference between a period and a semicolon might seem pedantic (well, it is), but it is still an interesting one. A literal transcription of the manuscript is incoherent.

> peculiar conscience ~~that has been attributed to Claggart.~~ ^assigned ~~as~~ to be the^ ~~we have insu inadequately descri discribed touched upon private mentor~~ of Claggart;
> And, for the rest, not improbably ~~he p~~ it put him upon new experiments. (https://app.textlab.org/transcriptions/15872?stage=StCa)

The text would be rendered as 'peculiar conscience assigned to be the of Claggart; And, for the rest, not improbably it put him upon new experiments', which is clearly wrong. The final 'And' phrase makes a stand-alone sentence, and the previous sentence implies an incomplete revision. Either way, an editor needs to make some changes. All editions have restored the deleted 'private mentor' because otherwise the phrase is incoherent. The decision to change the semicolon after Claggart to a period follows the logic that Melville intended to finish the manuscript leaf with a stand-alone sentence. NN keeps the semicolon and lowercases 'and'. The MEL editors concluded that the intention of the last (completed) sentence trumps the previous sentence that was unfinished. Bearing in mind that these simple changes affect the reading of the text (not just its meanings but its rhythms), editors still need to intervene in appropriate places.

But again, some editors may exploit the same logical crux from previous examples to make unnecessary changes. In chapter 27, for example, in which Melville wrote of Billy's burial, '*the last office* of the sea-undertakers, the Sail-Maker's Mates, were now speedily completed' (my emphasis). Hayford and Sealts and the NN edition emend to 'offices', attempting to align the phrase with the conventional phrase for the 'last rites' for the dead, and to make the subject agree with the plural verb. However, the singular 'last office' appears in chapter 28 of *Moby-Dick* (in a passage cited in the entry for 'last offices' in the *OED*): 'If ever Captain Ahab should be tranquilly laid out . . . then, whoever should do that last office for the dead, would find a birth-mark on him from crown to sole'. A plural verb seems to disagree with 'office', but the implication of the word is a ceremony consisting of several funeral obsequies given by several mates, so it is not confusing to see a plural verb. MEL retains Melville's original wording, and includes a pop-up note about the reasoning for leaving it alone as against previous editions.

As I mentioned in Section 2.1, editors of *Billy Budd* must also confront how to treat odd spellings, and these decisions can lead to critical insights. In chapter 30, for example, Melville wrote that the spar from which Billy hanged was venerated by sailors: 'Their knowledges followed it from ship to dock-yard and again from dock-yard to ship, still pursuing it even when at last reduced to a meer dock-yard boom'. That odd spelling of 'meer' (meaning 'mere') gives the reader pause, unless that reader were using the NN edition, which emends to 'mere'. I assume the NN editors made the change because Melville does use 'mere' elsewhere in the novella, so they are seeing this as a mistake to be corrected or a spelling to be regularised. Was it a mistake, though, considering that he spelled it correctly more than once elsewhere? The *OED* establishes 'meer' as an acceptable spelling up to the eighteenth century, which is when *Billy Budd* is set. A keen reader of Milton, Melville may have even recalled that same spelling in *Paradise Regained*, 'To the utmost of meer man both wise and good, / Not more'. The interpretive possibilities are lost when the editor changes Melville's tendency to use words in unusual, archaic, and artful ways; 'meer' also relates to both boundaries and water (relating as it does to the German *das Meer*), which are apt reminders of this sea-faring journey about the hazy boundaries between justice and injustice, and between land and sea (a theme that Melville explores elsewhere). The word 'meer' is the kind of anomaly that asks for a passing theory to adjust our understanding of Melville's text.

As Bryant wondered, when Melville wrote that Billy's 'face, lustrius with perspiration, beamed with barbaric good humor' in the first chapter, is it incumbent on the editor to (again) fix Melville's spelling?[120] Editors will never know for certain whether Melville misspelled 'lustrous' (or the archaic 'lustrious') on purpose or not, but at least consider that, like Keats, Melville revelled in wordplay and coinages and odd spellings. As against the spell-checking of previous editions, MEL keeps Melville's 'lustrius' spelling because it signifies a double meaning of shiny and glowing. This decision is meant to underscore the two options and to encourage readers to ponder the nature of difficult editorial problems with their own passing theories.

Even a clear reading text that accurately represents the manuscript can inhibit critical discoveries regarding Melville's intentions. Melville made late revisions to complicate Captain Vere, himself a *late* addition to the story, in *early and middle* chapters.[121] A crucial question about Vere involves justice – was Vere unjust in executing Billy, who was both guilty (in the sense of murdering Claggart, his superior) and innocent (in the sense of not meaning to do harm and having been bullied by Claggart)? As Melville revised, he transformed Vere from the dutiful Kantian to an unsettled executioner of Billy; later, the decision haunts his psyche. Vere,

---

[120] Bryant, 'Editing Melville in Manuscript', pp. 121–2.

[121] For an indispensable survey of the composition of *Billy Budd*, see Parker, *Reading* Billy Budd.

as an 'exceptional character' whose devotion to his service had nevertheless 'not resulted in absorbing and salting the entire man', exhibits a kind of injustice (in the sense of disproportion, a breaking of the balance) with a 'marked leaning toward everything intellectual', aligning himself 'toward those books to which every serious mind of superior order ... naturally inclines'. And, 'With minds less stored than his and less earnest, some officers of his rank, with whom at times he would necessarily consort, found him lacking in the companionable quality'.

All these passages were written at a late stage, and then subject to further pencil revisions: for example, the un-companionability phrase came after Melville replaced an entire leaf to rewrite his sense of Vere's imbalanced aloofness. Before Vere was a 'character' with more dramatic depth, he was merely a 'sea-officer', which he deleted and then tried 'man'. The narrator's question about Vere's mental state in chapter 20 ('Was he unhinged?') may be used to discredit the captain's handling of Billy's crime in subsequent chapters. But considering Melville's compositional stages, his documented reading of the pessimist philosopher Arthur Schopenhauer, and his correlation between madness and inspired wisdom, this development in Vere's character becomes less incriminating and Billy's fate less a result of Vere's failings than of tragic elements ingrained within the will of a superior intellect. Such a fatalistic reading is that Vere's 'lot was cast' – another passage that was inscribed in pencil at a late stage, as Figure 3 shows.[122]

Melville left a telling passage in chapter 28: 'Truth uncompromisingly told will always have its ragged edges; hence the conclusion of such a narration is apt to be less finished than an architectural finial'. Telling, in that the work is fable, yet it partakes of several historical facts in addition to truths about human nature and the nature of art. In no other Melville text does this aesthetic – and editorial – statement show better than in *Billy Budd*, his final work of fiction.

The NN and Hayford-Sealts editions of *Billy Budd* are remarkable achievements that were assembled by legends in scholarly editing. Any edited reading text in a printed form is useful, and any digital edition ideally builds upon prior editorial achievements (which is certainly true of MEL),

---

[122] See Wenke, 'Melville's Indirection'; Ohge, 'Melville's Late Reading'.

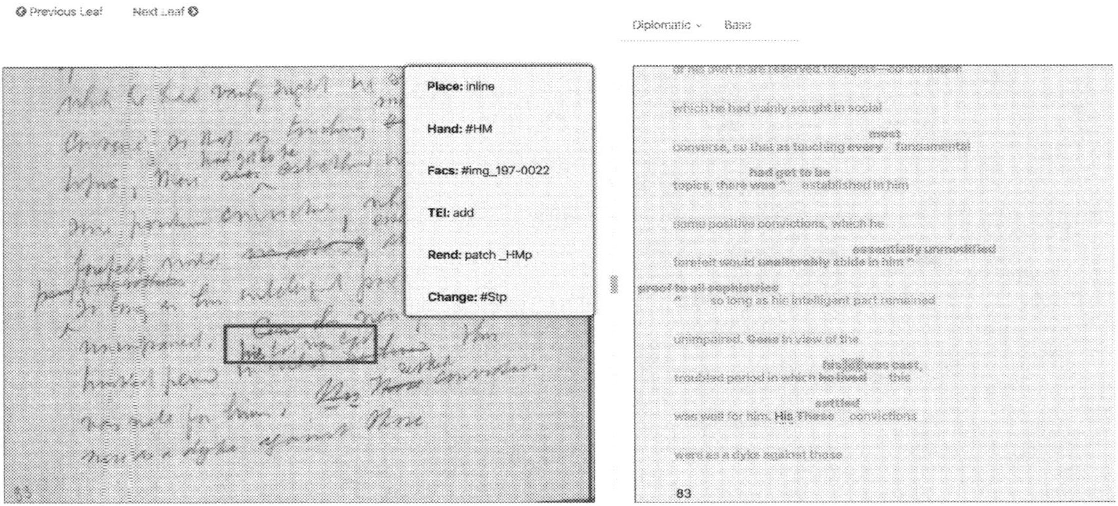

Figure 3 Manuscript revision in chapter 7 (leaf 197) of Melville's *Billy Budd* highlighting that Vere's 'lot was cast' (MEL, https://melville.electroniclibrary.org/editions/versions-of-billy-budd/chapter-7).

but print editions are limited by book technology and an incumbent set of assumptions about the nature of critical editing. Digital editing provides editors with more options to display more documents, navigate revisions, and invent technological strategies for showing those 'ragged edges' of a text, while aspiring to greater transparency, computational efficiency, and collaboration. Even if one were to disagree with the logic of MEL's editorial choices, the MEL text explains its rationale against other editions while it offers access to the *Billy Budd* manuscript and Melville's revision process. Demonstrating literary process-as-experimentation, the MEL edition seeks to meet the criteria of aesthetic experience: readers can have a direct engagement with the author's and the editors' thinking, and readers can take what they would like from multiple interfaces for experiencing the work.

3 The Data

3.1 Computation, Text Encoding, and Text Analysis

Editing and computation have always been interlinked; they both work on patterns. A pattern is a summary that permits you to generalise about data – what is to come next, or what would have come next. Patterns also allow us to neglect odd pieces of data (outliers), yet it is often the outliers to which the scholars attend in texts. Data is only a meaningful concept relative to a theory of what exists and how it came to be and who is collecting it. Data also comes with its own intentions – data is the product of human actions, packaged with a directedness to communicate something.[123] I want to preface this section by illustrating that the basis of 'computing' is intertwined with thinking, and how that thinking relates to digital practices towards literary data and editing. Various forms of data analysis can and should be a central aim and a distinguishing experimental feature of editions of experience.

The word 'computation' comes from the Latin *computus*, which was used well into the early modern period. It denotes various calculations, the most apt being the dating of the calendar for religious events. Scholars in the medieval era produced 'computus texts' for accurate dating. The visual representation of calendrical calculations in Figure 4 shows the interplay among text-based computing, reckoning, and the digital (digits, literally). The English noun form of 'compute' took on the analytical character of reckoning, indicating both a dating or calculation as well as an accounting of religious observance. In the sixteenth century, the verb form of 'compute' appeared for the first time. In the Renaissance imagination, the word 'machine' denoted ingenuity and mental processing, whereas the 'engine' denoted impersonality.[124] To 'compute' then started to mean an act of calculation, but intertwined with thinking, and turning thinking into tabulations. Thinking as a kind of reckoning by the machine.

---

[123] See also Gitelman, *"Raw Data" Is an Oxymoron*; Williams, *Data Action*.

[124] See Hyman, 'The Inner Lives of Renaissance Machines'.

Figure 4 Joseph ben Shem Tov ben Yeshu'a Hai's *She'erit Yosef [Joseph's Legacy]* (1804). © British Library Board, British Library, Or 9782, Folio 14 r (www.bl.uk/manuscripts/Viewer.aspx?ref=or_9782_f014r).

Shakespeare had an intuition about these nuances. Falstaff's catechism on the hollowness of 'honour' in Act V, scene 1, of *Henry IV, Part 1* makes a forceful point about the subtle confluence of calculation and language:

> Yea, but how if honour prick me off when I come on, how then? Can honour set to a leg? No. Or an arm? No. Or take away the grief of a wound? No. Honour hath no skill in surgery then? No. What is honour? A word. What is in that word honour? What is that honour? Air. A trim reckoning![125]

Honour is a kind of empty calculation for this calculating figure. The metaphorical computation results in a logic of duplicity – *if honour is meaningless, then it would be absurd to be injured or to die for it; therefore, I can pretend to be dead on the battlefield to avoid injury or death*. The master of duplicity and treachery, Richard III uses the only instance of 'computation' in Shakespeare's *oeuvre*, when relaying the story about his brother Edward V's illegitimate claim to the throne – this 'computation' is another kind of 'trim reckoning'.

> Tell them, when that my mother went with child
> Of that insatiate Edward, noble York
> My princely father then had wars in France,
> And by true computation of the time
> Found that the issue was not his begot . . .. (Act 3, scene 5)[126]

It is suggestive that the first quarto of the play (1597) published in Shakespeare's lifetime reads 'iust [just] computation', and that it became 'true' in the posthumously published First Folio (1623) – what should the editor choose, and for what reasons?

Quantitative approaches are inevitable in scholarly practice, and, as Martin Eve argues, they have long been essential to literary studies. Eve offers several examples of the 'quantifying urge' in literature, including

---

[125] Shakespeare, *Henry IV, Part I*, pp. 145–6.   [126] Shakespeare, *Richard III*, p. 287.

Vernon Lee's quantitative analyses in *The Handling of Words* (1923), courses at Dartmouth in 'Literary Analysis by Computer' in the late 1960s, and his own subject of the experimental novelist David Mitchell.[127] Other pioneers include Josephine Miles and Roberto Busa, who used computers to create linguistic analyses and concordances. Quantification is also used in editing: the frequency of an odd spelling, for example, may help the editor determine whether the author intended such a spelling or whether it was a typographical mistake that should be corrected. In authorship studies, the relative frequency of function words reveals an author's unique style. Eve contends that quantifying can be marshalled to enhance close reading. I can assert various statistical facts about Melville's work – for example, that various forms of 'reckoning' appear seven times in *Moby-Dick*, and a total of thirty-four times in eleven works, or that Melville even uses forms of the word 'compute' eight times throughout his work. These word frequencies generate questions about Melville's use of computation-words that are indebted to Shakespeare, an author we know Melville read. I arrive at this chain of new critical interpretations through digital computation (a corpus search of machine-readable documents),[128] as well as basic editorial and digital techniques (a corpus of texts, a concordance, ngram key-word-in-context lists).

The etymology of 'computation' suggests that computers are not machines but engines that create new directions of travel for readers. Humans are no longer the only readers; machines are, too, though machine reading is a different kind of reading – it is a kind of parsing based on human instructions, pattern recognition, and brute calculation. Editors must be open to the notion that computational reading can demonstrate discursive formations by changing the underlying structures of knowledge. Combining calculative and creative reasoning (or what Joseph Weizenbaum calls *deciding* versus *choosing*)[129] could reshape how we engage with and experience editions as computable data collections that

---

[127] Eve, *Close Reading with Computers*, pp. 2–3.

[128] See Thomas Anthony's AntConc tool for corpus research: www .laurenceanthony.net/software/antconc/.

[129] See Weizenbaum, *Computer Power and Human Reason*, pp. 11–13, 258–80.

generate new interpretations. An edition of this kind would not necessarily be published as a codex-like reading object but rather as a collection of data sets that can be computed (and reckoned) with text analysis tools.

Which brings me to text encoding and text analysis, and encoding *as* analysis: many researchers have practised text encoding and text analysis as separate tasks.[130] This split between editorial encoders and literary data analysts has even been reflected in their preferred data models: text encoders prefer hierarchical, semantic data models based on individual judgement, usually expressed in XML, whereas text analysts prefer unstructured plain text files that can be processed with programming languages. Is it necessary to encode semantic features of a text? For the text encoder, this question borders on blasphemy, yet I have heard several computational linguists say that semantic encoding is a waste of time because natural language processing (NLP), named entity recognition (NER), or a form of machine learning will reveal what matters in the text without our having to manually encode semantic information. Using a pragmatic approach means that the answer depends on the questions, but a complementary method of semantic encoding and programming that combines the instrumental and experiential would be most rewarding.

But what is text analysis and why do it in an editing project? Text analysis is fundamentally a computer-assisted calculation of word counts and various other statistics in a corpus (e.g. word and sentence lengths, lexical uniqueness, unique word frequencies, parts-of-speech tagging, average word use, sentiments, and topics). John F. Burrows once suggested that 'the real value of studying the common words rests on the fact that they constitute the underlying fabric of a text, a barely visible web that gives shape to whatever is being said'.[131] Computational analysis reveals an anatomy of text, or the dissection of literature into parts, as well as an understanding of the whole.

---

[130] The separateness of text encoding and text analysis was the subject of a panel at the 2012 Digital Humanities conference: www.dh2012.uni-hamburg.de/confer ence/programme/abstracts/text-analysis-meets-text-encoding.1.html.

[131] Burrows, 'Textual Analysis'. See also Burrows's study of Jane Austen, *Computation into Criticism*, and Jockers, *Macroanalysis*.

The divide between encoding and analysis is evident in the current MLA guidelines for scholarly editions, in which the words 'data mining' or 'text analysis' do not appear as essential criteria.[132] Hans Walter Gabler hints at the direction that editorial text analysis could take when he identifies the edition as 'both the product and the facilitator of scholarship and criticism', which 'enables analysis and generates knowledge in continuity'.[133] Tara Andrews also included 'analysis' in her four-part list of desiderata for digital editions (to a lesser extent, so has Peter Shillingsburg).[134] Even so, her criteria encourage the reduction of the customisation and flexibility that are essential to TEI encoders. Andrews advocates for more automation, systemisation, and programming skills of editors to facilitate analysis. While this perspective is valuable, I advocate a notion of analysis that aims to be more expansive, flexible, and geared to new ways of reading editions. Text encoding and analysis should be complementary activities because of the ways in which the analysis can reveal the 'barely visible' aspects of the edition. Analysis is not just the *how* of encoding; it is also the *why*, as well as the *what for* – the use of the edition's data. Analysis involves both the decisions for robust semantic markup that will facilitate text analysis and data mining, and the text analysis tools themselves that will provide further insight into the edition.

How do the theories of textual editing alluded to in the Introduction shape computational methodologies? Daniels and Thistlethwaite have asserted that '[d]igital technologies have radically altered the traditional

---

[132] For the MLA Guidelines: www.mla.org/Resources/Research/Surveys-Reports-and-Other-Documents/Publishing-and-Scholarship/Reports-from-the-MLA-Committee-on-Scholarly-Editions/Guidelines-for-Editors-of-Scholarly-Editions#editor. See also MLA's recent white paper on electronic editions, 'MLA Statement on the Scholarly Edition in the Digital Age': www.mla.org/content/download/52050/1810116/rptCSE16.pdf.

[133] Gabler, 'Theorizing the Digital Scholarly Edition', in *Text Genetics and Literary Modernism*, ww.openbookpublishers.com/htmlreader/978-1-78374-363-6/ch6.html#_idTextAnchor018.

[134] See Andrews, 'The Third Way'; Shillingsburg, *From Gutenberg to Google*, pp. 101–2.

structure of habits in the scholarly workflow'.[135] Pierazzo has also posed an important question: can the methodologies of editing 'be pursued digitally or does the digital medium necessarily provide a new theoretical framework'?[136] Pierazzo sets up a distinction between implementing old methods (and outputs) of editions versus creating a new methodology. While she leaves the question open, I have seen old methods inform digital editions while computational methods enhance what might be called the 'old' methods.

Digital editions are well placed to maximise the advantages afforded by enhanced memory and computational pattern recognition techniques that expand analogue reading experiences. Any editorial approach that minimises or closes off the possibilities of computation as a generator of new thinking will be just as perilous as a lack of historical awareness of the textual condition. Conceiving of the text as connective nodes of text, memory, and knowledge will facilitate new views on the edition against the background of what is known.[137] A balanced application of scholarly and statistical approaches to textual editing could generate new questions and directions for critical interpretation.

Why have textual editing and stylistics maintained a separation, especially as digital technologies have been central to both disciplines? One clue comes from my early historical and methodological survey about authorial intention. Editing focuses on intention, whereas stylistics, as a formalist discipline influenced by the 'intentional fallacy', did not even consider it.[138] But the time has now come to show how editorial and computational research can complement each other with digital methods. The confluence of editorial and analytical approaches requires a reckoning with data. Releasing data and using various interfaces for displaying data can be just

---

[135] Daniels and Thistlethwaite, 'Being a Scholar in the Digital Era', p. 9.

[136] Pierazzo, *Digital Scholarly Editing*, p. 15.

[137] A 'node' can mean XML elements (tags), specific attribute values within those tags, or the textual matter (the words contained within the tags), as well as an entity that connects to 'edges' in a network graph.

[138] Stockwell and Mahlberg, 'Mind-Modelling with Corpus Stylistics in *David Copperfield*', p. 129.

as effective as an interface that displays encoded documents, for example. But what exactly is data in the editorial world? Tiago Sousa Garcia has suggested that, for computer scientists, data is just a prima facie assumption of doing the work. Data can be misunderstood as merely a statement of fact. However, data is frightening for literary scholars, not just because statements of fact seem scientistic; yet data is created by humans with biases.[139] Text is another uncanny idea to computer scientists for whom a 'text' is a string of characters. Humans like to complicate things; computers do not. As Garcia put it:

> Text and data are not the same thing ... but they serve similar functions, and are treated in the same fashion, in both camps. The real barrier at the centre of this problem .... is an epistemological one. On the one side, the desire for clarity, exactness, uniquely defined categories, and one-faceted information; on the other, the love of fuzziness and ambiguity, the knowledge that the world is always more complicated than we think, and ultimately irreducible to human understanding ....[140]

One way they complicate things is by classifying data to make it useful – from counting to sorting, modelling to visualising, creating metadata fields to encoding annotations. 'What distinguishes data from other forms of information is that it can be processed by a computer, or by computer-like operations', and that data moves, as Miriam Posner and Lauren Klein put it.[141] Data information is then made to be tractable, in that it can be subject to efficient algorithmic processing. And tractability relies on mathematical processes; the labels we create are contingent. A pragmatic embrace of the epistemological gaps between data and text mindsets creates

---

[139] For more on humanities data and bias, see Drucker, 'Humanities Approaches to Graphical Display'.

[140] Garcia, 'Working Together', n.p.

[141] See Posner and Klein, 'Editor's Introduction: Data as Media'.

new opportunities for textual editors to attempt to straddle both sides of the debate, to aspire to broader inquiries.

The success of computational editing depends not just on the strategies for data entry and creating an interface to display text but also on the means by which underlying data can be analysed and visualised with computers. This capability is not necessarily about the 'front end' of the edition (the website); rather, it is about the data files that make up the edition: XML files, tables (in .csv or .tsv), data frames, images, and scripts in XSLT, JSON, JavaScript, Python, R, and other languages. By making texts machine-readable, we are halfway there, but any subsequent markup decisions also need to be guided by what will be queried through processing and analysis tools. The Women Writers Project, led by Julia Flanders at Northeastern University, has already put data analysis into practice with the Intertextual Networks Project and the release of an analysis interface for the Mary Moody Emerson digital edition.[142] Textual editing now includes the building of a computational model for digital publication as well as facilitating new ways of reading editions that are not possible in analogue formats.

The building of a computational pipeline should include decisions about the accessibility of data: digital editors should consider whether their XML data is amenable to the analysis of researchers from outside the project. Tim Berners-Lee has written about the five levels of open data specifications, encouraging the availability of data on the Web with an open licence, as open data, in a machine-readable structure (e.g. Excel instead of image scan of a table), in a non-proprietary format (e.g. CSV instead of Excel), and using open standards from W3C (RDF and SPARQL) to identify things, so that people can link to the data, to provide context.[143] This model, while

---

[142] For the Emerson project, see wwp.northeastern.edu/blog/new-visualization-almanacks/. The Jane Addams Papers Project has also created a prototype spatial network analysis of Addams's colleagues (https://digital.janeaddams.ramapo.edu/socialnetworks). See also Beshero-Bondar and Donovan-Condron, 'Modelling Mary Russell Mitford's Networks', for a report on a text analysis of The Digital Mitford project database.

[143] Berners-Lee, 'Linked Data'.

a useful guide, misses some of the complexities of even open-source, non-proprietary data. An edition might have a four-star rating of openness – it is available on the Web, it consists of machine-readable documents, it uses non-proprietary software, and it employs linked open data. But it is not 'open' in practice if a digital researcher needs a specialist's manual to figure out how to analyse the site's layers of data.

Regarding an open workflow, Gabriel Bodard and Simona Stoyanova have observed that 'the rigorous intellectual effort of indexing in a tradition[al] project is changed in the digital process, but not replaced by an automated process'.[144] Referring to the order in which these skills are taught in workshops on EpiDoc, they note that 'this structure follows the workflow of an epigraphic project, where the indices, tables of contents, lists of lemmata etc. are produced at the end of the project from the encoded XML files'. Thinking about the desired indices, tables of content, and other organisational features is best done at the earlier stages, to allow not only for planning the encoding that needs to be done in order to produce these features of the edition but also for establishing what else could be done beyond the markup itself. While the generation of indices might still be done at the end of a project, the thinking about what indices are needed is best done as early as possible. The same is true for the creation and structuring of internal authority lists such as place names and prosopographies (and/or identification of the relevant external authority lists), although inevitably these will be populated as the project progresses. It is always necessary to select the markup carefully: in a world where editors could encode almost any aspect of a text and its physical support, the time, funds, and expertise available will always be limiting factors. When I was helping to encode digital texts at the Mark Twain Project, we concentrated only on encoding basic structural features, textual apparatus, and metadata because the primary aim of this massive project was to present textual information, so there was no time left to encode character or place names. The digital workflow, then, must make choices about encoding features such as places, events, dates, individuals, names, commemorative relationships, age, social status, and occupation, depending on the focus of the project or that of its expected audience.

---

[144] Bodard and Stoyanova, 'Epigraphers and Encoders', p. 55.

Bodard and Stoyanova are also right to suggest that encoding should be taught alongside a programming language (for purposes such as linked open data (LOD) and NER) and text analysis tools such as Voyant and AntConc. Making researchers aware of the potential of corpus linguistic tools for editorial projects would help to bridge the gap between text encoding and analysis. Projects such as Recogito aim to produce user-friendly interfaces for the creation of LOD and NER, so that users can increase their confidence in at least some of these areas in a short learning time.[145]

A recent debate in textual scholarship between historical (or 'documentary') and critical ('copy-text') editors illustrates the importance of thinking in terms of encoding as analysis. One of the complaints about digital documentary editions – and their materialist cousins, genetic and versioning editions – is that they work for a small audience of specialist scholars.[146] Some of these editions are unreadable, at worst; many users want a clean, accurate reading text.[147] The problem with that argument is that it is forceful only in the context of codex- or document-based human reading processes. A versioning text, or a transcription of a revised and uncompleted manuscript, can be 'read' (that is, parsed) in a novel way with the tools of text analysis. Text analysis can be an adjunct to the normal reading process: Voyant Tools, for example, provides both a clear reading interface in addition to various visualisations and statistics of the text data (word clouds, graphs, data frames, and networks). The digital interface can make the reading process of difficult manuscripts smoother than that of their print predecessors by engaging the reader with the material context rather than relying on complex genetic symbols. One criticism levelled against the limited page-by-page transcription of a digital documentary edition like Jane Austen's Fiction Manuscripts does not consider the intellectual value that text analysis could bring to that edition's XML data. The problem that we might 'distance ourselves and our editions from the readers' is more of

---

[145] See Pelagios' Recogito tool for semantic annotation: https://recogito.pelagios.org/.

[146] For more on genetic editing, see Deppmann et al., *Genetic Criticism. Texts and Avant-textes*; van Hulle, *Textual Awareness*.

[147] Pierazzo, *Digital Scholarly Editing*, pp. 78–9.

an interface issue than a worry about the usefulness of the edition's data.[148]

Marginalia studies exemplify encoding as analysis, at the node level, which connects to the notion of experience and experimentation. Melville's Marginalia Online (MMO) is a virtual archive, bibliography, and searchable edition of Herman Melville's library. The encoding decisions in the initial phase of the project could have followed the TEI, but the aim of the project was to create a searchable database of Melville's markings and annotations that matched the word-level results with their corresponding digital surrogates. The resulting co-ordinate-capture XML encoding does just that:

```
<div id='2' x='277' y='2415' group='1' width='1299'
height='129' type='checkmark' sealts='460_1_c011'
attribution='HM' mode='comedy' play='1a'>
<w x='416'>That</w>
<w x='526'>this</w>
<w x='653'>lives</w>
<w x='726'>in</w>
<w x='815'>thy</w>
<w x='1023'>mind?</w>
<w x='1197'>What</w>
<w x='1344'>seest</w>
<w x='1469'>thou</w>
<w x='1574'>else</w>
<div id='3' x='277' y='2479' group='1' width='1075'
height='74' type='underline' sealts='460_1_c011'
attribution='HM' mode='comedy' play='1a'>
<w x='353'>In</w>
<w x='446'>the</w>
<w x='580'>dark</w>
<w x='836'>backward</w>
<w x='943'>and</w>
<w x='1124'>abysm</w>
<w x='1192'>of</w>
```

---

[148] Robinson, 'Toward a Theory of Digital Editions', pp. 126–7.

```
<w x='1345'>time?</w>
</div>
</div>
```

This is Melville's first marking (with an embedded additional marking) in *The Tempest*, from his seven-volume set of Shakespeare's plays that he was studying while composing *Moby-Dick*. Each instance of marginalia is contained within a <div>, which includes several attributes identifying various bibliographic and holographic information. This is not TEI-compliant, but it is functional as to its purpose, which is to enable word searches of marginalia with corresponding highlighting of search results in the digital facsimile of the page from Melville's book. TEI encoding would make it easier to refine some kinds of analysis (of, say, marginalia differences between poetry and prose structures), and the project has plans to incorporate TEI. Yet the fact that each instance of marginalia is encoded with a <div>, and that each <div> has additional attributes (such as the marking @type, the play's @mode, the play's @title, and the @sealts attribute, which identifies bibliographic information as well as the page number in a single value) means that the data is already amenable to text analysis. Also, each word encoded within a <w> allows for fine-grained markings-level and word-level analysis.

Complemented with the plan to encode Melville's marked texts were a series of XSLT and R scripts for performing text analyses on Melville's reading data. XSLT scripts created HTML tables of all the markings that could be sorted by word count. R code adapted from Jockers could run word frequency and linguistic calculations on the markings. Other R code using tidy text principles created sentiment analyses of Melville's marked content.[149] The illustrations and statistics resulting from the text analyses illustrate Melville's varying forms of engagement in his readings, clarifying hitherto un-analysed and under-appreciated aspects of his marginalia. Word frequencies illuminate ideas and

[149] See Rockwell and Sinclair, *Hermeneutica*; Jockers, *Text Analysis with R for Students of Literature*; Silge and Robinson, *Text Mining with R*.
The Programming Historian (https://programminghistorian.org/) also has tutorials on AntConc, Python, and R, among many other computing topics.

themes that interested him; lexical uniqueness and word-sentiment values of marked passages offer clues to the rhetoric and perspectives to which he gravitated. The visualisations of reading evidence bolster conceptions of the writers that influenced him. Text analysis does not always have to be concerned with large swaths of data; it can also bolster the reading of smaller data sets. The node-level text analyses showed the value of using text analysis techniques to complement the close reading of an edition. But the text analyses constitute both a form of new experience for a reader and a demonstration of experience via composition, as Melville's creative process of reading and annotating Shakespeare while writing *Moby-Dick* is now immediately accessible.

Consider, for example, a simple XSLT script I created to convert the XML-encoded marginalia into sortable tables. Authors who used these tables for the June 2018 special issue of *Leviathan* devoted to 'Melville's Hand' found it efficient to have all the markings in one searchable table with their associated metadata and word counts.[150] This snippet from the table (https://christopherohge.com/460-word-count-per-marking.html) of Shakespeare markings is sortable by word count, which is important for gauging Melville's attention to brevity.

Word counts of all Melville's markings in Shakespeare's plays

Each Marking Instance	Word Count ▾
candle-wasters; (460_1_c488, underline)	1
Now (460_2_2.005, underline)	1
Charbon (460_2_2.360, underline)	1
Poysam (460_2_2.360, underline)	1
dibble (460_3_3.065, underline)	1
spleeny (460_5_5.192, underline)	1
that, (460_6_6.127, underline)	1

---

[150] Ohge and Olsen-Smith, 'Digital Text Analysis at Melville's Marginalia Online', and Ohge et al., '"At the Axis of Reality"'.

Cont.

Each Marking Instance	Word Count ▾
great (460_6_6.296, strikethrough)	1
tyrant's (460_6_6.296, strikethrough)	1
Ingrateful (460_7_7.085, underline)	1
supplied (460_5_5.241, strikethrough)	1
His friends (460_1_c393, underline)	2
world's debate. (460_2_2.082, underline)	2
gorgeous east, (460_2_2.126, underline)	2
barbarous multitudes. (460_2_2.204, underline)	2

This digital analytical groundwork was paired with critical interpretations to show that Melville's marking patterns reflected his own commentary about the 'intuitive Truth' of craft and genius – what Melville described as Shakespeare's 'short quick probings at the very axis of reality'.[151] Shakespeare's rhetorical stealth, Melville implies, comes with philosophically bleak implications. It is no surprise, then, that our analysis revealed that Melville's average word count per marking was lowest in Shakespeare's tragedies, and highest in the comedies.

Partnering with Performant Software, MMO has recently launched a complementary analysis interface, based on Voyant Tools, which shows general statistics of reading data. For example, Figure 5 visualises all of Melville's marginalia in his two-volume set of Milton, with each word result linking back to the Search Catalog and page images.

These data visualisations illustrate a confluence of pragmatic, bibliographic, and computational thinking. Marginalia in books are pre-digital forms of hyperlinking that can be realised in the digital space for various analytical and experiential purposes. As Alessio Antonini, Francesca Benatti, and Sally Blackburn-Daniels have argued, marginalia are 'links to be' and 'links to the future', showing that authors use marginalia to

---

[151] Melville, 'Hawthorne and His Mosses', in *The Piazza Tales*, p. 244.

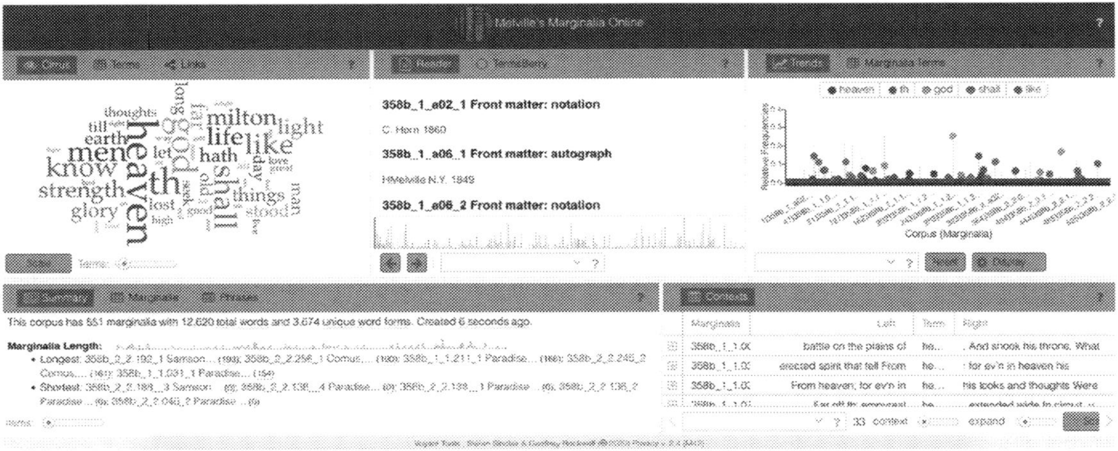

Figure 5 Visualisation of Melville's marginalia in John Milton's *Poetical Works*. Courtesy Melville's Marginalia Online (http://melvillesmarginalia.org/).

connect what they read to what they will write by highlighting what can be relevant to the form, content, or knowledge of the future work.[152] This kind of data will be of interest to stylometry scholars, as well as to other communities in literary and bibliographic studies.

The fragmentary nature of marginalia makes text analysis an essential tool for understanding Melville's creative engagement with his books. Such creativity amounts to experience, but the MMO digital interface invites readers to apprehend and engage with Melville's intellectual and creative process. Just as Emerson demonstrated a method of composition of journaling to lecturing to essay writing, Melville also experimented with a creative method of reading and annotating.[153] Readers can then have their own experiences realised through these processes of text-making.

Planning for the use of analytical tools, alongside decisions about how the encoding could be designed to facilitate further analysis, will make for more robust and accessible editions. Encoding and analysis is an iterative process, not least because experimentation is an important aspect of text analysis: researchers have their own questions and priorities, but editorial encoding itself is a form of close reading that will generate new questions and modifications. Including text analysis into editorial planning circumvents a long-standing problem in editions encoded in TEI: the text analysis produces computational results of the text *on the editor's terms*. TEI's flexibility is a strength, but, as I explore in detail in Chapter 4 and the Conclusion, that strength can also become a weakness if users want access to other projects' edition file(s) for their own text analysis. It would be preferable for a user to analyse editions themselves; when that is not practicable (owing to, for example, a complicated encoding customisation), the editor could provide a directory that makes analysis easier, or a pared-down file of the parts of the edition that should be analysed, or the analysis tools themselves.

An encoding-and-analysis method also entails that even minimal encoding could be marshalled to facilitate analysis, interpretation, and experimentation. For example, suppose that an editor wanted to create an edition

---

[152] Antonini, Benatti, and Blackburn-Daniels, 'On Links To Be'.

[153] Grimstad, *Experience and Experimental Writing*, pp. 27–8.

that marked all moments of religious allusion, and to create visualisations of those allusions across the edition, then the editor would be using analytical TEI elements that would then be subjected to scripts that process their occurrence.[154] I have seen other projects that produce an edition that encodes only one element (quotes, for example) across a large corpus so that linguistic analyses can be applied only to quotations. Even an accurate . txt file of a text that can be processed with a programming language or visualised with a tool such as Voyant can be very useful.

The minimalist idea is attractive because no one researcher will be able to do all the transcriptions, create a computational pipeline, write scripts in programming languages, and design a database and website – a selected team of professionals with complementary skills would be needed to bring all those pieces together. Yet it is crucial that digital editors model a workflow that is committed to encoding (even if it is minimal), while also being aware of how other digital researchers might access the project data for data analysis and visualisation. Any project will have its share of false starts and ill-judged decisions that lead to redoing some work, and these 'failures' are helpful to document in themselves.

In addition to encoding and text analysis, new experiments using machine learning, spatial networks, social network analysis, and 3D modelling will advance the field.[155] Editors should embrace change and learn new technologies as they develop. Such an openness to experimentation would also revive the original idea of the edition as an exhibition, or a production – an open-ended learning tool for texts. In practice, this means that publishing an edition would entail a range of options: a minimalist option could be releasing a collection of reliable .txt or .xml files that can be uploaded to Voyant Tools or AntConc or processed with Python NLTK or R TidyText tools; a maximalist option could consist of data with rich TEI encoding that can be published alongside various visualisations.

---

[154] For TEI analysis elements, see chapter 17 of the *TEI Guidelines*: www.tei-c.org /release/doc/tei-p5-doc/en/html/AI.html.

[155] See the special issue on Digital Scholarly Editing in the *International Journal of Digital Humanities* 1.2 (July 2019): https://link.springer.com/journal/42803/ volumes-and-issues/1-2.

3.2 Exhibition 2: Mary Anne Rawson's Anti-Slavery Anthology
The Bow in the Cloud *(1834)*

Some archival collections demand a new kind of editorial treatment. One such example is an anti-slavery literature anthology, *The Bow in the Cloud*, which employs a complementary method of text encoding as text analysis, as well as passing theories of intentionality. Published in 1834 by the London firm Jackson & Walford, the anthology collected ninety poems and prose pieces by a mixture of well-known and non-professional writers involved in anti-slavery societies throughout Great Britain. It was edited by Mary Anne Rawson, a founding member of the Sheffield Ladies Anti-Slavery Society, who sought to create what she called in her Preface to the anthology 'a structure of moral and literary architecture'. What also requires further study is the nature of the enterprise itself: this is an anthology, edited by a pioneering woman with specific aims that were complicated to articulate, at a crucial time in history. Attending to what Tom Mole calls the dynamic cultural practices of 'selecting, abridging, excerpting, framing, and mediating' of texts shows 'the power of anthologies to shape how their readers read'.[156] *The Bow in the Cloud* demonstrates unique practices for several reasons: it is an early example of the political literary anthology, and a rather large one (at 400 pages) with some long pieces, and it features grassroots activists, politicians, and well-known literary writers (but no Romantic authors, although Rawson tried to commission their work, as I will explore later). This kind of eclectic book not only reflected growing literacy rates in the UK but also was the product of several decades of energy from various publishing movements, including the religious press, the new business of editorial reproductions, cheaper printing technologies, and the expansion of the literary marketplace after the era of radical political publishing.[157]

The Bow in the Cloud also comes with an under-researched manuscript collection of more than 600 items that is vast and revealing – particularly so for an anthology of this kind, with so many contributors. Each submission

---

[156] Mole, *What the Victorians Made of Romanticism*, p. 188.

[157] See Wood, 'Radical Publishing', and Price, *The Anthology and the Rise of the Novel*.

to the anthology came with a covering letter (and some submissions have multiple letters spanning from 1826 to 1834), and some pieces also came with photographs, artworks, engravings, or newspaper clippings. The poems that Rawson chose to publish were also copied in her own hand, and several of those fair copies show evidence of her revisions to the pieces before she supplied a printer's copy to the publisher. Paying attention to these neglected documents makes it possible to discern Rawson's rationale for connecting with her target audience, and to see how her choice of material mediated anti-slavery rhetoric at a crucial time when the British were passing the 1833 Slavery Abolition Act and the American abolitionist movement, led by William Lloyd Garrison, were publishing their highest volume of print material. The focus on Rawson's editorial rationale presents a challenge to editors: it combines aspects of several editorial approaches, including the documentary, genetic text, and social text theories, yet it also adopts a principle of Rawson's editorial intentions using a logic similar to a critical editor's. Instead of focusing on the authorial intentions of the writers in the anthology, I follow Rawson's editorial judgements as the anchor for textual decision-making. The fact that the book is a multi-author literary anthology also presents new challenges to an editor. At the same time, the documentary and book historical focus requires attention to how the book was made and disseminated.

The manuscript collection, housed at the John Rylands Library, University of Manchester, has been digitised only recently, with support from the John Rylands Research Institute.[158] The digital images of the surviving manuscripts and visual material total 818 high-resolution files with extensive metadata of each item, based on my study of the manuscripts, as open-access images on an IIIF image viewer.[159] The surviving

---

[158] The collection is part of the Rawson/Wilson Anti-Slavery Papers, English MS 414 and 415, John Rylands Library.

[159] The *Bow in the Cloud* Digital Collection is available at www.digitalcollections .manchester.ac.uk/collections/bowinthecloud/37. IIIF (https://iiif.io/) is the International Image Interoperability Framework, an open source standard for image sharing.

evidence now being brought out will give the best sense yet of this unique volume's textual history. A digital edition with complementary analysis tools aims to bring out more of these connections in this under-appreciated anthology.

Let's consider that there are two revised drafts of Rawson's Preface. Each draft also includes unpublished notes. Like the *Billy Budd* digital edition at MEL, the transcriptions of *The Bow in the Cloud* manuscripts are encoded in XML using TEI guidelines (http://tei-c.org/). The markup identifies several useful genetic attributes, including the date of the manuscript, who made what changes, and other information about those changes and the medium. It also matches the transcription to its location on the page image. Figure 6 shows the opening of Rawson's Preface in the TextLab editing environment. Figure 7 shows the diplomatic transcription preview interface. Notice that one substitution – 'truth' for 'fact' – in Rawson's second draft, which illustrates the care with which she approached her introduction to the higher truths of the anti-slavery pieces she published.

One striking unpublished note from the Preface reveals Rawson's struggle to justify her role before the public:

> The Editor of this little volume is not placed in the awkward predicament of many original writers, who feel it necessary to make an apology for (appearing before the public) or (for adding to the number of books already before the public). She has no apology to offer – nay – so far from feeling one needful and pleading for indulgence, she is enabled to take far higher ground – she feels that she has conferred a favour on the public especially the junior part of it, and she can unhesitating[ly] say, that she considers [these] a *most valuable* & rare collection of original papers. . .

Rawson chose not to sign her Preface in the published version, so her 'role' was as an anonymous editor from Wincobank Hall, Sheffield. Her name does not appear anywhere in the published book.

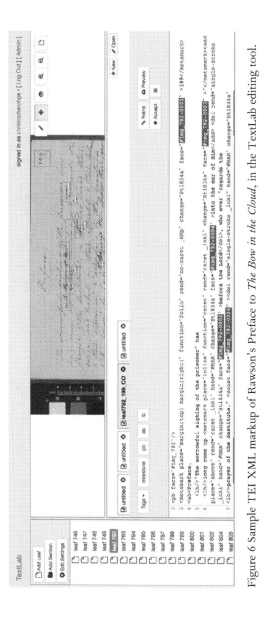

Figure 6 Sample TEI XML markup of Rawson's Preface to *The Bow in the Cloud*, in the TextLab editing tool.

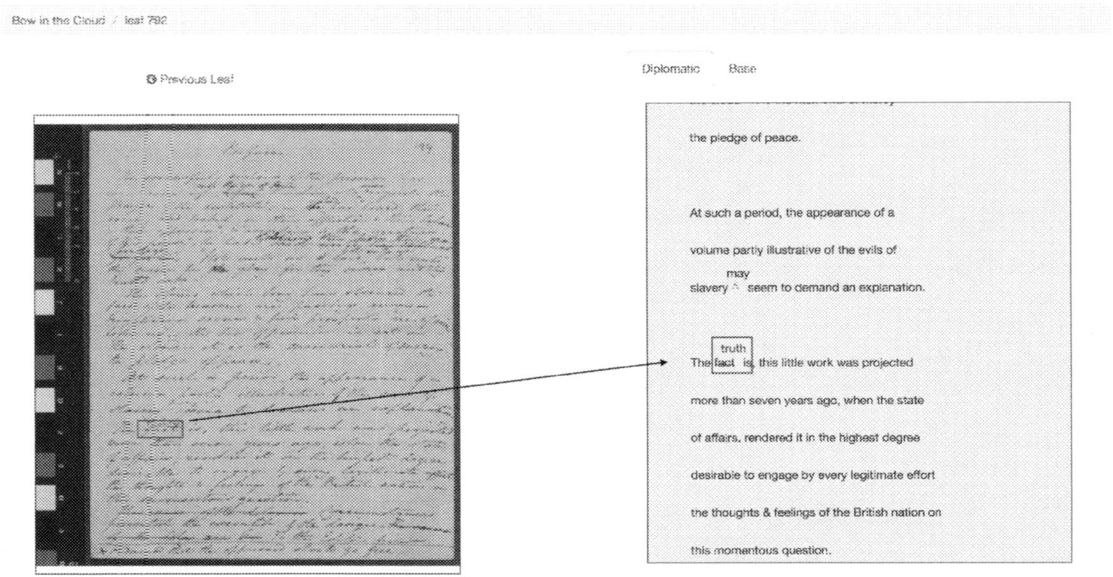
Bow in the Cloud
Previous Leaf
Diplomatic
Base
the pledge of peace.
At such a period, the appearance of a
volume partly illustrative of the evils of
may
slavery ^ seem to demand an explanation.
truth
The fact is, this little work was projected
more than seven years ago, when the state
of affairs, rendered it in the highest degree
desirable to engage by every legitimate effort
the thoughts & feelings of the British nation on
this momentous question.

Figure 7 Diplomatic transcription of Rawson's Preface to *The Bow in the Cloud*, in the TextLab editing tool.

These encoded documents consist not only of poem and prose fair copies (many of which were revised by Rawson) but also of the original submissions with their contributors' cover letters. Encoding of unpublished documents gives researchers a sense of the varieties of work and information exchange that went into the publishing of this anthology, as well as the connections among the documents that will form the basis of network analysis tools. For example, the prototype profusion graph of the manuscript catalogue shown in Figure 8 visualises the people who were associated with Rawson's work, and how much material they sent her.[160]

Rawson also solicited advice from some of the volume's contributors about the Preface and other contributors' pieces. One such clue left in the archive comes from the congregationalist minister J. W. H. Pritchard's letter from 11 April 1834. It proves not only that he helped her edit some poems in the book but also that he offered suggestions to Rawson's Preface, which were adopted. Pritchard wrote in one instance: 'The sentence [in the Preface] might admit of a change of this kind "It would indeed have been delightful if every hand which has taken a prominent part [or been actively employed] in pulling down the prison house, & in striking off the fetters of the bondsmen, could have put &c"'.

That phrase, as it was published on page 5 of the anthology, adopted some of his suggestions: 'It would indeed have been delightful if *every* hand which has been actively engaged in pulling down the prison-house, and striking off the fetters of the bondman, could have put a stone into the monument here erected upon its ruins, to tell posterity where it stood, the curses it contained, and how it fell'. This phrase is not in the two surviving drafts of the Preface. There was an additional printer's copy of the Preface, which does not survive, because there are still notable differences between the manuscripts in the collection and the published version. Her unpublished notes also show that she sent proof sheets to at least seven other readers.

While some of the poems submitted to Rawson were unchanged between submission and publication, there are many others that show

---

[160] See the Project's GitHub repository: https://github.com/cmohge1/bow-in-the-cloud-edition.

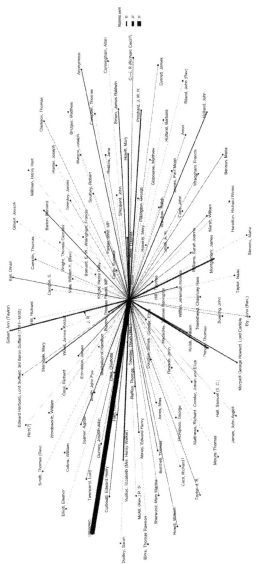

Figure 8 Dispersion graph of *The Bow in the Cloud* manuscript archive (https://christopherohge.com/presentations/bic-network-static-vis.jpg).

a significant level of Rawson's editorial engagement. For example, Rawson received four submissions from liberal Quaker poet Bernard Barton between 1826 and 1833, two of which began and ended the volume, and two more which appeared elsewhere in the volume. This suggests an attention to selection that is then confirmed by a note towards the end of the manuscript collection that shows Rawson outlining where some of the authors should be placed. It is also significant that the second piece in the collection is by Scottish poet James Montgomery, who was one of the best-known writers published in this volume, other than Ann Gilbert, Thomas Pringle, Thomas Buxton, MP, and Lord Morpeth. Montgomery's submission entitled 'Leonard Dober' is a historical fiction about the first Christian missionary to the West Indies, the German Johann Leonhard Dober. This piece exists in two versions and includes many substantive revisions. As was her practice, Rawson produced a fair copy of Montgomery's manuscript submission, and she would either confer with the author about further changes or she would make local changes in her fair copy. Visualising the variance between documents is an analytical aspect of digital editing that changes the reader's experience.

Thinking of digital editing as a pragmatic method of encoding and analysis could illuminate experience through the anthology's wider social connections not only to other archival materials but also to other anti-slavery activists. For example, the sanguine verse that started to appear between the British 1807 Slave Trade Act and the 1833 Slavery Abolition Act, such as Montgomery's *The West Indies and Other Poems* (1823), came with a less celebratory tone in *The Bow in the Cloud*. Montgomery's Moravianism is an under-explored strand of the transatlantic religious map of British abolitionism. He connects to European and US anti-slavery through the poetry of Lydia Huntley Sigourney, who published a collection of poems about the Moravian Count Zinzendorff in 1835. In 'Leonard Dober', Montgomery narrates the Moravians' first evangelical mission to the West Indies, in 1732, to convert black slaves. Religion in general has been underplayed in recent histories of anti-slavery, so this piece also shows how nonconformist sects steered the anti-slavery debate. Montgomery is a guiding light in this collection in other ways, too, for many of the contributors were friendly with him or had worked with him (as was the case with Rawson). In one of his letters to Rawson, he advises her on how to edit some poems in the collection.

Several other instances of Rawson's direct influence on the original manuscript submissions prove her active engagement. One of the more striking examples is the printing of an extract from a letter, 'Compensation for the Slave', from the prominent Quaker and abolitionist MP Thomas Buxton. Buxton's submission came in a 6 October 1833 letter to Rawson at the end of which Buxton admits, 'you are of course at liberty' to include and emend his contribution. The printed first line is not the same as the extract in his letter. In her fair copy of his extract, Rawson proceeded to revise sections of it as she went through it and added some pencil revisions towards the end of the process.

Yet she was not satisfied with it. On the last page of her fair copy of Thomas Pringle's poem 'The Wild Forester', as Figure 9 shows, she copied the first half of Buxton's letter extract in pencil and added further revisions which were adopted in the published version. About half of the published version of Buxton's letter extract turns out to have been rewritten by Rawson.

Thomas Pringle furnished some of the most revealing manuscript evidence in this collection. Pringle was a Scottish poet who is best known for writing some of the first English poetry about South Africa; among his admirers were Samuel Taylor Coleridge, who said that Pringle's 'Afar in the Desert' was a masterpiece of lyric. As acting secretary to the Anti-Slavery Society in London, Pringle was well-connected in the literary and political world. Pringle corresponded with Rawson in late 1833 as he sent her his poems and attempted to connect her with other writers.

Pringle's letters (six in all) in the archive show an energetic activist who helped Rawson guide this collection into print. What was not known until now is that Pringle advocated to Rawson in a 20 June 1833 letter to delay bringing out the volume. A week later, on 27 June 1833, Pringle was the signatory of the published proclamation of the Act of Abolition. (On 23 August 1833, Parliament passed the bill.) This helps to explain Rawson's difficulty in writing her final Preface – what was left to be

Figure 9 Rawson's pencil revisions to Thomas Buxton's 'Compensation for the Slave' prose extract in *The Bow in the Cloud*. John Rylands Library, English MS 415/146a (www.digitalcollections.manchester.ac.uk/view/ MS-ENGLISH-00415-00146-A/3). (CC BY-NC 4.0)

done, after full abolition in Britain? Pringle encouraged Rawson to change the focus of the anthology to a 'commemorative' book because they were about to achieve one of their primary legislative aims. Yet the manuscript archive shows more tension between commemoration and activism to achieve a *universal* abolition of slavery.

There are many other similar examples of collaboration between Rawson and her authors, but her omissions are just as revealing. This is evident in Dinah Ball's work. Ball was Rawson's former governess in charge of educating Mary Anne and her sisters, but she had also published poems in newspapers at this time. She submitted two poems to Rawson: one, titled 'Hope', appeared in the collection, but anonymously; yet her other poem was not printed, possibly because it glorified Toussaint L'Ouverture's violent revolution in Haiti. It is a pity that the thirty-two-stanza poem on seven manuscript pages was left out.[161] There are other compelling instances of omissions in the volume that illustrate Rawson's editorial judgement. Ann (née Taylor) Gilbert, the well-regarded children's poet who often co-wrote with her sister Jane Taylor, sent a poem that was published as 'The Mother' (she is listed in the volume as 'Mrs. Gilbert'). Her submission came with a small watercolour illustration (see Figure 10) that Rawson did not use. All three of Gilbert's poems in the volume examine the pathos of shattered domesticity created by slavery. These illustrations are unique examples of the wealth of archival material in the collection that had been difficult to access before the collection was digitised in 2019.

Two tragic poems by Sarah J. Williams were not included – they were written as a diptych, titled 'The Planter's Last Hour' and 'The Slave's Last Hour'. The poem of hers that was included, 'A Voice from the Land of Bondage', was also subject to Rawson's editing: as Figure 11 and 12 show, the first three stanzas were left out. The poem's opening stanza in manuscript is striking: 'The die was cast' parallels the language of the third line, 'To fix the date' – suggesting a tension of what is to be determined after such injustices.

---

[161] See Ferguson, *Subject to Others*, pp. 269–70.

The first three stanzas were probably expurgated owing to their fatalist tone, as well as the presence of the slave's anger and revenge. The published version begins with the manuscript's fourth stanza.

Figure 10 Ann Gilbert's ('Mrs. Gilbert') unpublished illustration to 'The Mother' *(The Bow in the Cloud)*. John Rylands Library, English MS 415/152+ (www.digitalcollections.manchester.ac.uk/view/MS-ENGLISH-00415-00152-A/1). (CC BY-NC 4.0)

Stanza I, MS

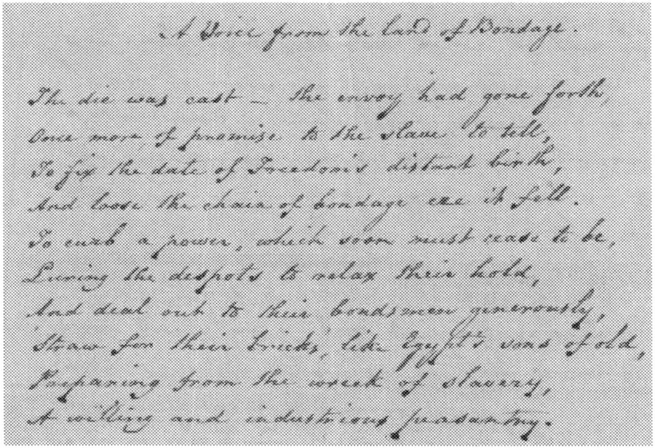

A Voice from the Land of Bondage.

The die was cast – the envoy had gone forth,
Once more of promise to the slave to tell,
To fix the date of Freedom's distant birth,
And loose the chain of bondage ere it fell.
To curb a power, which soon must cease to be,
Luring the despots to relax their hold,
And deal out to their bondsmen generously,
Straw for their bricks, like Egypt's sons of old,
Preparing from the wreck of slavery,
A willing and industrious peasantry.

Figure 11 The first stanza of Sarah J. Williams's manuscript submission, 'A Voice from the Land of Bondage' (*The Bow in the Cloud*, https://www.digitalcollections.manchester.ac.uk/view/MS-ENGLISH-00415-00127/1). John Rylands Library, English MS 415/127. (CC BY-NC 4.0).

Stanza 3, MS

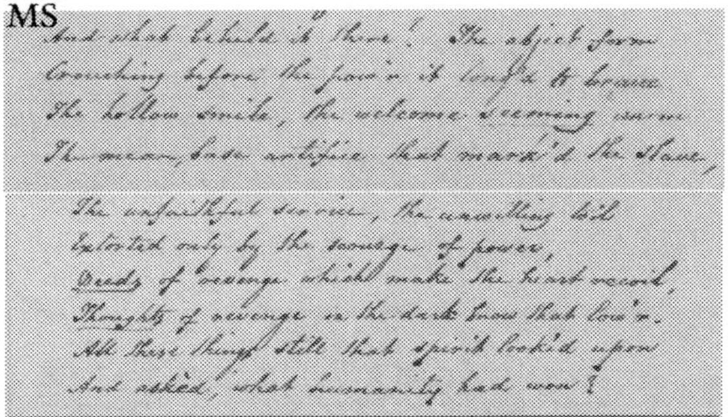

And what beheld it there? The abject formation
Crouching before the pow'r it long'd to brave
The hollow smile, the welcome *seeming* warm
The mean, base artifice that mark'd the slave,
The unfaithful service, the unwilling toil
Extorted only by the scourge of power,
Deeds of revenge which make the heart recoil,
Thoughts of revenge in the dark brow that low'r,
All these things still that spirit look'd upon
And asked, what humanity had won?

Stanza 4, MS

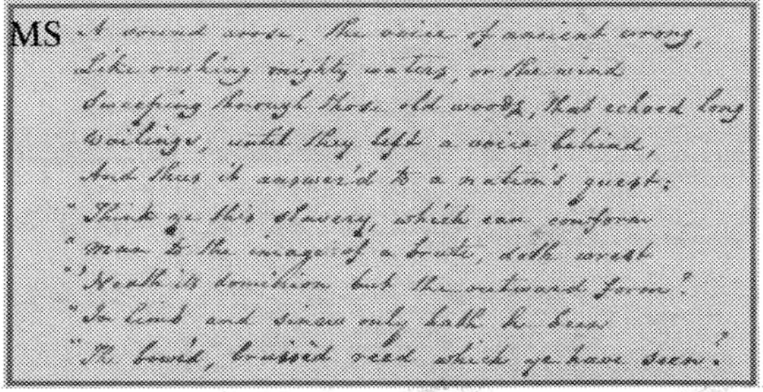

[First stanza in the published version]

Figure 12 The third and fourth stanzas of Sarah J. Williams's manuscript submission, 'A Voice from the Land of Bondage' (*The Bow in the Cloud*, https://www.digitalcollections.manchester.ac.uk/view/MS-ENGLISH-00415-00127/1). John Rylands Library, English MS 415/127. (CC BY-NC 4.0).

> A sound arose,– the voice of ancient wrong,
> Like rushing mighty waters, or the wind
> Sweeping through those old woods, that echoed long
> Wailings, until they left a voice behind . . .

The poem loses its force when the emotional build-up in the previous three stanzas is extracted.

Another poem that was not included was by James Everett, entitled 'A Reign of Terror'. In his 1826 cover letter to the poem, he justified the 'simple form of expression' in the long poem thus: 'I could view Slavery in no other light than that of one continued system of oppression and terror,' and stated his aim to be 'more of *strength* than of *ease*'. After his stark criticisms of the law, the penultimate stanza of his poem eerily predicts, 'And judgment, though it linger long, / Will burst in wrath for Afric's wrong, / And now begins to move.' Here is the final stanza:

> Away, – for down the fabric falls
> The voice of blood for justice calls,
> And God in Vengeance reigns.

There are two practices here that merit attention: Rawson's intentional actions to not publish this poem (and others like it) in 1834, but also to save it, come with an assumption that someday someone would be able to understand the range of emotions that this anthology elicited.

Rawson's collection, as published, was representative of the abolitionist movement at this time, featuring religious leaders, politicians, non-professional writers, and writers of repute. Among those who declined, however, are prominent names such as William Wordsworth, Robert Southey, Thomas Moore, Thomas Babington Macaulay, and the father of the abolitionist movement Thomas Clarkson. Wordsworth's letter declining to contribute indicates that slavery is 'on principle monstrous, but it is not the worst thing in human nature', suggesting that the purpose of poetry is to stand above immediate political concerns: 'Poetry, if good for any thing, must appeal forcibly to the Imagination and the feelings; but what at this period we want above every thing, is patient examination and sober judgement'. He also expressed concern for the unintended consequences that would accompany a 'hasty' (as he called it) abolition: '[T]here are three parties – the Slave – the Slave owner – and the imperial Parliament, or rather the people of the British Islands, acting through that Organ. Surely the course at present pursued is hasty, intemperate, and likely to lead to gross injustice'. Wordsworth's letter was included in Alan G. Hill's Oxford edition of his letters (volume 5, 1979), but an edition of this anthology shows the broader context of Wordsworth's decision not to participate in this literary event.

One of the most intriguing letters comes from John Clare. From his cottage in Helpston, he wrote a lengthy response to Rawson's initial invitation of 1826. This letter has never been published in full; it was not included in Mark Storey's Oxford edition of Clare's letters (1986) and is quoted partially in Jonathan Bate's *John Clare* (2003). Neither of these, however, would be able to show the letter in the context of its purpose – Clare's contributing a poem to the anthology:

> I am sure Slavery is an abominable traffic & a disgrace to Mahomedism much more Christianity for it is utterly at variance with religion & nature ... I have never heard of the Work you mention as I am but seldom applied to for such matters in fact I live in such an unknown corner of the Country that a letter hardly finds out the way to me unless directed as above then there is often some difficulty but I hope this will find you to assure you that I am ever anxious to assist in every laudable endeavour as far as my humble abilitys will permit me.

He never sent a poem – another unfortunate omission.

The publisher, Jackson & Walford, was also responsible for the *Eclectic Review*, the *Congregational Year Books*, and other ecclesiastical books. One of the contributors to *The Bow in the Cloud*, Josiah Conder, had since 1813 been the owner and editor of the *Eclectic Review*, which also featured a substantial and laudatory review of *The Bow in the Cloud* in its July 1834 issue. This review was significant, since the *Eclectic Review* was one of the most prestigious literary periodicals of its time, one that published not only prominent romantic authors but also American authors such as Washington Irving. It was not long after the publication of *The Bow in the Cloud* that American abolitionists William Lloyd Garrison and Frederick Douglass visited Rawson and several of her peers, illustrating the significance of this figure and her noble attempt to influence public opinion through the force of literature and transatlantic networks.[162] Rawson's publication comes directly at the moment in 1834 when, as Richard Huzzey has argued, the British started to use 'anti-slavery' as a national credo that projected moral superiority over other civilisations.[163] Yet Rawson's anthology, and particularly the cache of unpublished material she decided to save, shows that she was aware that such posturing was far from altruistic or compassionate, as new forms of violence and economic exploitation of colonial possessions continued to be central to British foreign policy and British allies.

These hitherto undocumented details surrounding Rawson's editing of the anthology show her as an active editor, organiser, and writer. Rawson relied on her social network of anti-slavery activists, through the Sheffield Ladies Anti-Slavery Society but also in London and elsewhere. The details are also data and statistics that could aid researchers: text mining the published anthology reveals some intriguing leads – for example, 'liberty' is used more frequently (103 times) than 'freedom' (74). The word 'power' is not a common word, relatively; various forms of 'equal' occur only nineteen times, and 'equality' does not occur at all. Yet in an unpublished 10 May 1833 letter from William Marsh, in the archive, he asserts his belief that, like any Englishman, any African slave should be 'actually free, & knows that his children will be the same & that he can speak his mind without the fear of the lashes that he cannot ever be struck with impunity, & that he partakes, equally with his superiors, of the protection of the Law'. These words also have connections that are hiding in archives waiting to be revealed through computation and contextualisation. The word 'liberty' often co-occurs with

---

[162] See Brown, 'William Lloyd Garrison'; McDaniel, *The Problem of Democracy in the Age of Slavery.*

[163] See Huzzey, *Freedom Burning.*

'word', 'love', and 'free' (why not with 'God' or 'action' or 'law', for example?). Such dynamic aspects of meaning and textual production can be enhanced with TEI XML encoding of the manuscripts. Rawson's editorial project is therefore more than the sum of its bibliographical facts or its data model – the networks of the archive, the data and their statistical valence as well as the inclusions and omissions surrounding Rawson's editorial vision also merit consideration. *The Bow in the Cloud* edition is pragmatic because the material suggests a focus on the book's genesis as well as the data connected to the publishing of a physical book – the nodes of which can be illustrated, analysed, and networked with computation and digital publication. Whereas the *Billy Budd* edition draws attention to the unfinished manuscript, *The Bow in the Cloud* uses the manuscript evidence to draw attention to the editor of the anthology and the nature of the printed book as a significant event within networks of print culture. Rawson's example illustrates the shift from what editing *is* to what it *does*, as it is not solely *object-based* but rather *activity-based*, focusing as it does on various roles of authors, editors, works, and readers existing within complex relationships which are subject to various rules of publishing an anthology in the 1830s.

This network-oriented edition is currently using the semantic web authoring tool Scalar (http://scalar.me/anvc/features/web-standards/) to publish the front end of the project. A Scalar project might be modelled as a 'book', but it offers a wider range of possibilities than a printed book. The platform assembles media from multiple sources and juxtaposes them with narrative and metadata using linked open data structures (exportable into RDF XML, a prominent standard for linked open data). Images, annotations, and tags are rendered as *paths*, which are arranged as pages with *relationships* – that is, linear sequences of content that can intersect and nest (like paragraphs in a chapter, chapters in a book, and so on). It combines *linear* and *non-linear* paths, achieving a balance between standardisation (common vocabularies of metadata standards) and flexibility (free text tagging, annotations, and narratives). Integrating IIIF (https://iiif.io/) images of *The Bow in the Cloud* manuscripts also ensures interconnectivity and long-term viability. Everything in the platform (images, annotations, tags) is a page that relates to other pages in a network, as is evident by this prototype network graph of archival image tags (see Figures 13 and 14).

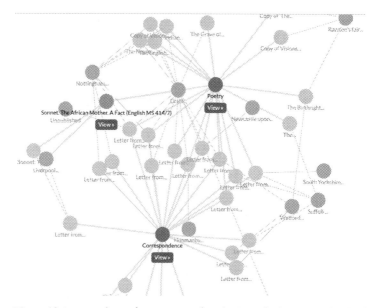

Figure 13 A network graph prototype of a selection of *The Bow in the Cloud* manuscripts rendered in Scalar.

Clicking on 'View' on the individual node of, for example, 'Sonnet. The African Mother. A Fact' (top left of Figure 13) gives the reader more information about this item written by Jane Roscoe, the wife of the leading abolitionist and Unitarian William Roscoe (Figure 14).

A collection of digital facsimiles with substantial metadata, complemented with a network graph that shows their connections, is alone a significant tool for inquiry – a tool that does not necessarily require transcriptions to be effective. The edition of this anthology aspires to model a digital museum of archival experience, through a digital reconstruction of encoded texts from its archive, and a broad consideration of literary, archival, and socio-political networks. This curated experience starts with an annotated reading text based on the book and moves through an exhibition of facsimiles of archival materials

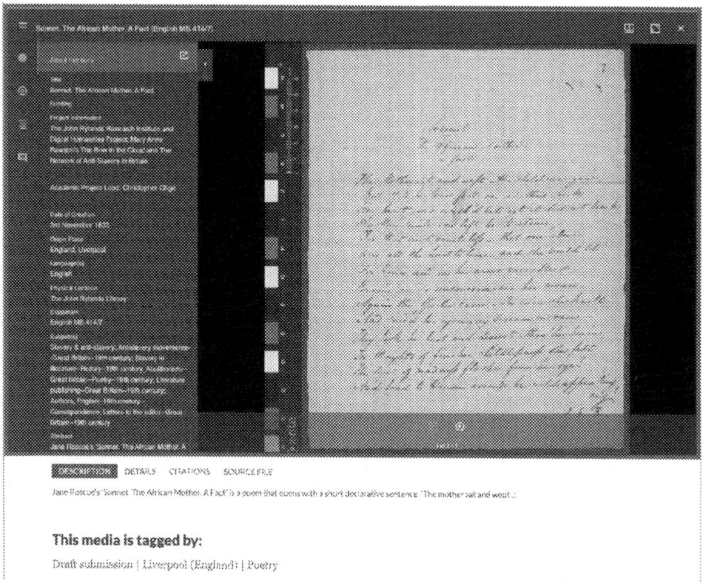

Figure 14 A tagged IIIF media page of the manuscript of 'Sonnet. The African Mother' in Scalar.

in the network. As Ruth Ahnert, Sebastian E. Ahnert, Catherine Nicole Coleman, and Scott B. Weingart have shown, network analysis allows us 'to measure the relationships between many entities in multiple ways, allowing a rich, multidimensional reading of complex systems never possible before'.[164] Unlike *Billy Budd*, *The Bow in the Cloud* is more of an archival recovery project of a *publishing event*. As more scholars move beyond the constraints of single-author editions, examples like the Rawson project will present new opportunities for scholarly experimentation with the diverse voices in our archives.[165]

---

[164] Ahnert et al., *The Network Turn*, p. 7.
[165] See, e.g., Ozment, 'A Rationale for Feminist Bibliography'.

4 The Edition

4.1 Moving beyond Editorial Bookishness

Gilbert Ryle's evaluation of Peter Nidditch's Clarendon edition of John Locke yields a mixture of relevant insights about the forms of editions. Ryle, a philosopher, decried the irrelevance of the apparatus, which includes a lengthy appendix that exhaustively catalogues the 'patois of the printing-house'.[166] The jargon of the publishing trade and myriad trivial variants populating the textual apparatus, according to Ryle, distract from the main goal of the project: to help readers better understand Locke's *Essay on Human Understanding*. Print technology after Gutenberg has mostly eliminated scribal problems: the desire to approximate, however imperfectly, the finally intended text is a holdover from a classical era where originals were lost and authoritative texts were reconstructed by comparing flawed copies of their lost originals (the archetype). Yet many editors of the critical-eclectic school continued an anachronistic search for an archetype of a text finally intended yet never actually realised. What Locke originally wrote was not lost, it was printed. It was later revised, and posterior revisions do not suggest that the editor should try to recover some lost version that was uncorrupted by print. Ryle intuited that Nidditch was privileging editorial conventions over a useful edition of Locke.

Scholarly editors have long been criticised for printing documentation that seems indulgent and even unnecessary – for example, a long list of line-end hyphenations, or unreadable genetic transcriptions with complicated notation systems. Such documentation may be unnecessary for many readers, at best, or at worst illustrate what Kingsley Amis satirised as a 'funereal parade of yawn-enforcing facts' with 'pseudo-light' thrown onto 'non-problems'.[167] Editors do need to provide lists, but the question is, what lists are useful to whom? Ryle suggests that the editor should make principled decisions about what is worth attending to. The product of critical editing, the printed clear reading text, conceals from readers the

---

[166] Ryle, 'John Locke Re-edited', p. 1043. I thank Simon Blackburn for suggesting Ryle's review.

[167] Amis, *Lucky Jim*, p. 14.

processes and bibliographic facts underlying texts, relegating change, corruption, and other aspects of transmission into a list or other apparatus elsewhere in the book. 'Grotesque systems of notation are developed in order to facilitate negotiation through labyrinthine textual scenes', McGann once observed about a 'postmodern incunable' print edition.[168] John Lavagnino has called attention to the problem of two audiences – on the one hand, a scholarly audience with background knowledge in editing and bibliography, and on the other, a 'general' audience that requires reliable texts made by editors but that may not understand the scholarly apparatus.[169] Textual and contextual apparatus is still often made to satisfy the narrow demands of other scholarly editors, not the readers who would learn useful information about the work. Lavagnino suggests that editions should provide critical points of view for texts that are aimed at several distinct kinds of user. Henry James once said: 'No theory is kind to us that cheats us of *seeing*'; likewise, no editorial theory is kind to readers if it deprives them of seeing literary experience.[170]

Such a pragmatic sense of vision and openness recalls Dewey's foundational principles on the freedom of the will in education:

> [T]he task of the educator is threefold. First, to keep alive plasticity, initiative, capacity to vary; to prevent induration and fixation in fossilized automatic habits. ... Secondly, to confirm preferences; to build up and strengthen positive and constructive interests in specific directions. ... Thirdly, to make preferences *reasonable*; that is to say, to develop in individuals the habit of forecasting the consequences of acting upon a given preferential tendency, of comparing one set of results with another, and by these means enlightening preference as its own deeper and more abiding nature.[171]

[168] McGann, 'Editing as a Theoretical Pursuit', in *Radiant Textuality*, p. 79.

[169] See Lavagnino, 'Access'.

[170] James, 12 January 1891 letter to Robert Louis Stevenson, in Edel (ed.), *Henry James: The Selected Letters*, p. 242.

[171] Dewey, *The Middle Works*, p. 466.

Freedom invokes praxis – the fruit of teaching (Philip Sidney) – not a nebulous abstraction. Dewey would later clarify that freedom meant 'that kind of interaction which maintains an environment in which human desire and choice count for something'.[172] Eco also associated meaning with freedom – a freedom for readers to determine their own boundaries of experience with art.[173] But what are the boundaries of the digital edition? I see the educational as well as the ethical implications of creating 'an environment' of digital archives in which texts enable choice, flexible habits, and enhanced powers of analysis, appreciation, and plasticity.

How can scholars create a better environment for experiencing textual inventions? The answer – and a complicated one at that – is that we need to publish digital editions and continue to experiment with technology. One way to bridge the gap between the two audiences would be to pursue a continuity between the technical and the aesthetic through our editing of digital texts.[174] This brings me back to experience – the dual nature of experience being immersion in literary composition and experimentation, and the interdependent communities accessing that experience by attending to the literary work in various media (which will inevitably involve some elements of play, failure, and surprise).[175]

MEL editors, for example, use a fluid text approach that combines practices of genetic and critical editing. Yet even if we grant that texts are fluid, the notion that 'all versions are created equal' does not end the debate on how to publish an edition.[176] Readers might be encountering a 'fluid text', but they are not *experiencing* fluidity any more than one can experience the fluidity of a specific bend in the river or of a flower in bloom. I would venture to say that it is impossible to experience fluidity in any meaningful way, particularly if the versions are so myriad as to be unintelligible. A fluid text is still constrained by finite instantiations, and it still needs restraint in

[172] Dewey, *Human Nature and Conduct*, p. 10.

[173] See Eco, '*The Open Work* (1989)'.

[174] McCarthy and Wright, *Technology as Experience*, pp. 193–4. I return to this theme again in the Conclusion.

[175] See Ramsey, 'The Hermeneutics of Screwing Around', pp. 111–30.

[176] Bryant, *The Fluid Text*, pp. 17, 47.

terms of how the text can be meaningfully edited, or the data meaningfully processed, for user needs.

Mary-Anne Rawson's *Bow in the Cloud* anthology generates new principles of editing, yet it also uses technology to effect selective principles of historical-documentary, genetic, and social text editing. For other works, such as Mark Twain's late works, I may end up using a manuscript-based eclectic approach because we have evidence of Twain's biographer modifying his work after his death. It depends on the documents and the intended audience: the issue, as Tanselle says, is 'when to be eclectic, how much departure from a documentary form of a work is allowable and desirable, whether editors should introduce emendations of their own in addition to readings drawn from other texts, and what principles or standards should underlie alterations of either kind'.[177] Yet Tanselle does not say that facts, prior theories, and interpretations interpenetrate and undergird those 'principles and standards'. Emerson's 'wise skepticism' and what the philosopher Susanna Rinard has deemed a 'pragmatic skepticism'[178] suggest that editors have good reasons to make knowledge claims and to proceed with their work while granting that there may not be any truth underlying the claims of an 'author' or the 'final intention' or the 'work'.[179] Pragmatic scepticism amounts to a focus on literary practices as they have been enacted in writing and publishing that bring readers towards what Dewey called 'the nature of the production of works of art and of their enjoyment in perception'.[180] An interplay between the content of literature and the phenomenology of experience enriches aesthetic appreciation, which is, to quote Peter Lamarque, 'revealed by the complexity of the characterization of the intentional content of the experience'.[181]

A pragmatic digital edition can uniquely 'share evidence, advance considerations, and try to coordinate our views about things' in order to 'try to come to one mind about things', while emphasising the 'interlocking nature

---

[177] Tanselle, 'Historicism and Critical Editing', p. 14.

[178] Rinard, 'Pragmatic Skepticism'.

[179] Emerson, 'Montaigne; or the Skeptic', in Cramer (ed.), *The Portable Emerson*, p. 339.

[180] Dewey, *Art and Experience*, p. 11. [181] Lamarque, *Work and Object*, p. 138.

of systems of belief'.[182] Editorial judgements of documents or texts are not 'given' to unschooled minds but are, rather, interpretations of those materials. 'Gladly we would anchor, but the anchorage is quicksand', Emerson said.[183] These judgements demand a web of beliefs, not standing on bedrock but treading on a bog, as Peirce put it.[184] Experience and eventual verification require a process of refining and improving belief as editors and readers establish principles about publishing texts of works. The edition is meant to provide not answers but examples; to expose interesting problems, not to smooth over difficulties. The edition then becomes a radical new tool 'whose center is everywhere and circumference nowhere'.[185]

Now for the complications: continuing to think of the 'scholarly edition' as only a book- or document-like project in print and digital obscures the essential connotations of *editio* – the expansive idea that editions are exhibitions or productions of texts and networks, not merely a collection of documents assembled in a book. It is a collection of data to be stored and processed into interfaces; it is a corpus to be mined and queried by users; it is information asking to be curated by scholarship for meanings and experiences. An exhibition includes books and screens, narratives and images, linear and non-linear pathways, and multiple avenues of understanding. Editions could then be reconceived as digital *objects* that promote interlinked experiments of learning from literature – making them open-ended, fluid objects that are situated within creative pursuits and what Mikhail Bakhtin called the dialogicity of literature. Such a dialogical relationship among computing machines, individuals, and communities of practice will generate various insights, confirmations, and surprises. As with passing theories of intentionality, each person brings a history to interactions with texts and technologies that changes, and is changed by, experience.

Compromises still need to be made. Pragmatism promotes continuity between the intellectual (theoretical) and the practice-based (technological) sides of editing. Instead of adopting tech-solutionism (thinking that

---

[182] Blackburn, *Truth*, p. 39.

[183] Emerson, 'Experience', in Cramer (ed.), *The Portable Emerson*, p. 263.

[184] Referenced in Blackburn, *Truth*, p. 40.

[185] Rorty, *Consequences of Pragmatism*, p. 70.

technology alone will solve editorial problems), or reducing the experience of editing and reading into abstract categories, I contend that technologies, like theories, contain maxims that come with trade-offs. The editorial principles alluded to above – historical, eclectic, genetic, social editing – are *framing devices* for creating data models, and these decisions come with their own semantic and structural limitations which ultimately affect the published products. Experience is a matter not of corresponding with essential truths but of an ongoing attunement to the process of understanding and experimentation – a process which needs to be framed, and a framing which needs information technology. This leaves editors and readers with ample opportunities to use data models to inspire new critical approaches and vocabularies of appreciation.[186]

4.2 Data Models and Data Experience

The editor's choice of data modelling also requires pragmatism as it should be based on a variety of practical factors: what the material requires, what data model can best communicate the scholarship, what structural and semantic features should be recorded, and how much time and resources would be required. Another feature, however, is that modelling itself is a pragmatic, iterative process. In his book *Statistical Control* (1997), co-authored with Alberto Luceño, George Box repeated his polemic that 'all models are wrong, but some are useful', and added the pragmatic proviso that 'any model is at best a useful fiction – there never was, or ever will be, an exactly normal distribution or an exact linear relationship. Nevertheless, enormous progress has been made by entertaining such fictions and using them as approximations'.[187] Data models now dictate the methods of editing documents. At best, these useful fictions can be deployed as enhanced databases. But what is a document? A document is a system of ordered hierarchical objects, some digital editors would tell you. It is a plain text file containing strings of characters, another group of linguists or data analysts might say. Ted Nelson has said that a document is a 'construction of ideas,

---

[186] In addition to alluding to Rorty, I am also echoing Feslki, *The Limits of Critique*, p. 150.

[187] Box and Luceño, *Statistical Control*, p. 6.

created by human minds for human minds', concluding that '[i]f we leave
the design of the documents to the techies, they will screw it up, and that is
exactly what has happened'.[188] Nelson is thinking with both
a computational and a pragmatic framework; documents reflect human
biases and assumptions, and those must be reduced to a model using rational
principles to be computed; but they are not prima facie rational models of
what there is in the textual condition.

It is not in my scope to analyse modelling in depth – modelling is its own
subfield, and I do not believe one needs to be an expert in data modelling or
statistical methods in order to produce compelling digital research.[189]
Modelling can seem misleading or intimidating in its use of schema and
complicated flowcharts, suggesting that the data model is a picture,
a representation of facts, a simplification of the object (the edition). It is
inherently reductionist, and that is why models are forceful – and sometimes useful – when they are coherent. They are wrong partly because the
internal logic of a model can never fully represent the material objects, and
their underlying social conditions, that are being modelled. All hypotheses
and theories will be subject to revision in the future. As Richard Jean So has
argued, digital researchers should not be afraid of being wrong and inves-
tigating how a model produces mistakes.[190] Any experienced modeller in
the humanities will warn you that the model is flexible and iterative –
I would add only that models are also incomplete and biased. This is not to
deny the utility of models, but rather, as Katherine Bode put it, to combine
modelling with 'book history's methodological pragmatism' to create
a robust digital research paradigm.[191] If models are framed as a rational
telos (i.e., describing a formal condition to which we should aspire), then
they will inevitably belie the fluid, holistic nature of speech and texts (and
scientific knowledge, for that matter).[192] Modelling is a pragmatic means by

---

[188] See also Nelson, 'A Cosmology for a Different Computer Universe
Infrastructure'.

[189] See Scheinfeld, 'Sunset for Ideology, Sunrise for Methodology?'.

[190] So, 'All Models Are Wrong'. [191] Bode, *Reading by Numbers*, p. 8.

[192] Putnam, *Pragmatism*, pp. 63–4. This also recalls Frank Ramsey's critique of
'scholasticism', 'the essence of which is treating what is vague as if it were

which fluid literary materials are both made computable and computed, engaging with evidence of computational corpus construction and historical context to refine understanding. That activity needs to be grounded in the framing devices provided by editorial and bibliographic principles. Elsewhere, in relation to computational literary studies, Bode argues that scholars should 'consider the nature of ontological gaps and epistemological biases in its evidence' by being grounded in 'a bibliographical and editorial understanding of literary works as distributed across . . . a vast network of specific material objects'.[193] The existence of more machine-readable and reliable textual data enables a better understanding of the 'shape' of literary history.

Editors could explore the creative tensions between modelling and editing by moving away from *rationalism* and towards *practice* in digital research. The computer scientists John McCarthy and Peter Wright have argued that computational rationalism needs to be balanced with practical and aesthetic concerns in human–computer interaction. 'The turn to practice came about because rationalism had created an obstacle to thinking about technology by reifying technological artefacts as objects of study apart from their making and use.'[194] Rationalism becomes stultified when the theoretical strategy is 'transformed into an ontological commitment'.[195] Textual scholarship has tended towards rationalism since the eras of philology and copy-text theory, and in the digital era it has added modelling to its rationalist theorising; positivist philology risks becoming techsolutionism.[196] Formalism is necessary for computing, but prescribing privileged data models and overcomplicating them comes with dangers. This means that not every semantic feature of the text should be in the data

precise and trying to fit it into an exact logical category', quoted in Misak, *Frank Ramsey*, p. 277.

[193] Bode, 'Why You Can't Model Away Bias'. See also Piper *Enumerations*; Underwood, *Distant Horizons*.

[194] McCarthy and Wright, *Technology as Experience*, p. 26.   [195] Ibid., p. 27.

[196] On editorial rationalism and pluralism, see Shillingsburg, *From Gutenberg to Google*, p. 182. See also McCarty, 'Modelling the Actual, Simulating the Possible'.

model. Many users are coming to an edition looking for some specific information, not browsing without preconceptions. Thinking of modelling editions as *what texts do* and *what they need* (rather than what they are), editors can study the making and use of texts as experimental projects that were enacted by human beings with histories and needs. Using a pragmatic frame of editing and modelling that is focused on practice, editors could achieve a balance of the gains of codex-style reading, bibliographic facts, and interactive, interconnected digital tools and archives. This framework corresponds to William James's idea of 'double-barrelled' experience, suggesting, as Dewey writes, that there is 'no division between act and material, subject and object, but contains them both in an unanalyzed totality'.[197] Aesthetic experience makes the mind alive to the complexities of texts and the promises of making and using them.

In practice, one way for a textual editor to account for experience would be to share multiple data formats instead of trying to control the user's experience through one privileged interface. Releasing textual data in a minimal format means that users could download the project files, analyse them using their own tools and processes, add their own encoding if they wish, and republish the data elsewhere or send it back to the originating scholar(s) for feedback. Another solution would be to encourage editors to publish multiple formats for various experiences such that users *can take possession* of the edition. For example, MEL has recently changed its software architecture. It is now a static website that works and looks nearly the same as it did when it was a dynamic website. Now users can not only engage with the website but also visit the project's GitHub site and download a copy of the entire site on their local machine for their own purposes. Or they could fork the GitHub repository and make their own modifications to the data. They can also access the XML files of the editions and upload them into a tool such as Voyant Tools for a different kind of text mining experience. Readers can not only take possession of MEL but also take its data and import it into various existing tools for different consummatory experiences. But MEL's primary site is also a site of experience because it offers multiple pathways for engaging with Melville's experiments with literature, and editors' practices of

---

[197] Dewey, *Experience and Nature*, p. 11.

analysing his creative process. Rather than seeing the site as a passive object, like a television screen, we follow Tim Berners-Lee's principle that Web spaces ought to be 'less of a television channel and more of an interactive sea of shared knowledge'.[198]

As digital editors translate data modelling into practice, and practice back into modelling, they must develop a coherent strategy for text encoding, which is the basis of making texts machine readable (computable). Most courses and workshops would encourage editors to use the TEI guidelines expressed in XML. As I said in the Introduction, I have taught many of these workshops myself. The TEI standards reflect the current consensus of a digital editing community which has existed since the late 1980s. TEI's flexible guidelines were built with what James Cummings called a 'pragmatic level of indirection which enables the standard to be used by vastly different editorial communities'.[199] They are driven not by commercial needs but by the scholars who make editions, and are also more flexible than they are given credit for: if editors find that something is missing from the TEI guidelines, they can create their own elements or attributes to suit their needs. If their modified TEI guidelines are applied consistently and the XML is well formed, it is valid. There is a reason that the TEI guidelines are not called the TEI laws. Conceived as pragmatic guidelines, the TEI is a collection of agreed-upon vocabularies that editors can use to model their work.

The advantages of TEI XML notwithstanding, any XML encoder still needs to contend with a caveat that it is not a generalised solution to editorial problems or to primary data archiving; nor is it a data format that lends itself to easy publication.[200] While the TEI XML is the most pragmatic method of encoding scholarly documents, it is not the most pragmatic method of *publishing* them. Sometimes TEI is even impracticable and inadvisable. Consider the following final stanza from Tennyson's late

---

[198] Berners-Lee, 'Hypertext and Our Collective Destiny'.

[199] Cummings, 'Opening the Book', p. 185.

[200] In 'Beyond Gutenberg', Sandy and David Schloen argue that TEI represents 'secondary formats for communicating a particular reading of a text that has been generated from a richer underlying representation'.

version of his poem 'Early Spring', in manuscript. From a data modelling perspective, this stanza can be represented using TEI XML poetry elements:

```
<lg type="sextet" n="7">
<label>VII</label>
<l>For now the Heavenly Power</l>
<l>Makes all things new,</l>
<l>And melts the rime, and fills</l>
<l>The flower with dew;</l>
<l>The blackbirds have their wills,</l>
<l>The poets too.</l>
</lg>
```

The <l> elements are the result of a descriptive data model, yet the above poem in TEI could use three different tags for lines of poetry: <l>, <line>, or <lb/>. The first two are nearly synonymous line elements, except the second one is typically used for manuscript editing. The third is an 'empty' line break element (it does not contain any text). All three could be correctly deployed in a TEI XML file of a poem, but after being processed into HTML, all those lines become contained in <p>s. Encoded interpretations in data models are contingent and incomplete, as Fazi has suggested.[201] Any assertion of 'facts' about any text cannot be located, for they are interpretations which consist of beliefs about a situation.[202]

Most digital editors argue that all markup is interpretive. It is not uncommon to see statements such as 'the digital organisation and markup of such editions is just as much a product of the editor's interpretation and explicit intentions'.[203] There are interpretations that generate more consensus than others, and, as I said in Chapter 2, passing theories of interpretation hold when there is a consensus that coheres with the intentions evident in the author's text. There are also different modes of interpretation.[204] That a poem

---

[201] See Fazi, *Contingent Computation*.

[202] About locating facts, see Blackburn, *Truth*, p. 13.

[203] Rasmussen, 'Reading or Using a Digital Edition?'.

[204] J. Levinson, 'Two Notions of Interpretation', quoted in Lamarque, *Work and Object*, p. 163.

contains line groups, each of which contains lines, and which may or may not have rhyme schemes, is *determinative*. That a poem has metaphors or inter-textual or historical resonances is *exploratory*, being more interested in cognitive play than in concrete intellectual pay-offs regarding the text itself. TEI can encode both determinative and exploratory interpretations, but in my experience most projects' encoding is determinative. One reason is that exploratory encoding is time-consuming and subjective, and for publications the more structural encoding takes precedence. The other reason is that data structure itself may not be able to handle both: if one were to attend to other kinds of features of the poem – say, linguistic features such as phrases, rhyme scheme, and figurative language – alongside bibliographic features, one runs the risk of having 'broken' XML because of overlapping structures.[205] Nevertheless, it is determinative encoding that often gets lost in the transfor-mation to HTML, while exploratory or analytical encoding is better suited for criticism or a visualisation tool.

An XML model represents what a text *is meant to be* (what language we use in describing such things), whereas an HTML model represents what a text *appears to be*. Some digital editors see individualised data models as an advantage, as they are putting complex scholarly interpretations in the data rather than in the application or interface. The pragmatist position is that nearly all distinctions are inherently invidious, and any attempt to create a hierarchy among types belies the fact that literary texts are polyvalent. I am not suggesting that one model is better than the other, but rather that a pragmatic model would account for the advantages and disadvantages of each model's affordances for creating an experience. What is gained and lost by focusing your scholarly attention on *meanings* versus *appearances* of texts, and which tactic is most beneficial to readers?

Some critics of TEI have said that XML is hindering progress because of its strict hierarchies and massive tag set, but those criticisms ignore the fact that TEI can be implemented in any language and constrained using customisation. You could also eschew XML altogether and use a TEI

---

[205] See McGann, *Radiant Textuality*, pp. 174–5, 185–6. See also Sperberg-McQueen, 'Representing Concurrent Document Structures Using Trojan Horse Markup'.

vocabulary in JSON or TAGML, which encodes multiple text 'layers' with a graph-based data model.[206] But you could also encode a text in Markdown, render it in HTML, add semantic annotation within @class attributes or <span> tags using TEI vocabulary, and colour code words with semantic information in the browser. Alternatively, Web Components now allow HTML templates with custom element APIs (application programming interfaces) rendered in the browser that could theoretically replace TEI XML and place semantic tagging into the client side of processing.

TEI has survived for several decades owing to its widespread use and functionality in exemplary projects, but many of those projects have been supported by large grants or teams of dedicated staff to facilitate publication. Many scholars still find TEI too difficult and desire a simpler encoding system (a view which recalls Nelson's criticism of the 'techies' taking over the design of the documents). TEI documents include significant semantic information and features, and processing is required to transform all those features in the XML into another presentation format. Such a range of interpretations in data not only hinders interoperability but also creates more barriers to providing scalable publishing solutions.

The question is not whether one should use TEI XML or any other forms of markup but under what conditions should a project employ a TEI XML data model over another, and for what purposes? Hugh Cayless has often said that there is always a trade-off: either you pay now or you pay later. If a project needs fine-grained indexing of elements such as textual variants, people, places, dates, and other analytical features, as well as sophisticated metadata and linked open data, then TEI is a good option. But that project will need to accept that publishing and maintaining the edition or archive will be difficult and expensive. They will need substantial support from staff with expertise in XML, XSLT, RDF, databases, and front-end web development, and maintenance costs are likely to be several thousand pounds per year, *not* including staff time. On the other hand, if an individual scholar wants to transcribe a cache of manuscripts to be

---

[206] On TAGML, see https://github.com/HuygensING/alexandria. See also Dekker et al., 'TAGML'.

searchable and downloadable to complement new research in a published article, then there may be no good reason to use TEI in the first instance; a Markdown-to-HTML workflow on GitHub Pages, and archived on Zenodo with a DOI, would suffice because publication is much easier. TEI encoding could be a later step after funding is secured.

To address these complications, I now start my digital editing courses with Markdown, a minimalist markup system which was designed to deal with the problem of 'writing in' HTML by making document authoring and basic markup quick and simple.[207] Markdown also gives students the opportunity to consider the broad concept of digital 'markup' (which dates back to the 1960s, although 'markup' actually dates back to early modern printing) to build up their confidence, preview their editing, and put the focus on asking questions of the documents under consideration first, before moving on to extensible markup with TEI. Many editorial enterprises could stand to benefit from a minimum viable product approach that encourages publishing minimalist scholarly data first. As the minimal computing advocate Alex Gil has put it, the cost of maintenance

> continues to be one of the main reasons web projects fall by the wayside, or the reason you may be having a hard time getting your library to 'support' you in the creation and maintenance of your digital humanities project. These complex systems also demand more computation, increasing our collective carbon footprint [and] . . . makes these websites slower to access in areas of the world with low-bandwith.[208]

Creating static web assets may seem simplistic, but they provide access to rigorous scholarly information to more people using fewer resources.

---

[207] On Markdown, developed by John Gruber, see https://daringfireball.net/projects/markdown/.

[208] Gil, 'How (and Why) to Generate a Static Website Using Jekyll, Part 1'. See also http://go-dh.github.io/mincomp/.

The idea behind minimal computing is to bundle encoded text files into static, non-database-reliant assets that can be easily archived as well as published using Jekyll, Hugo, or GitHub Pages.[209] Suppose I am interested in publishing a group of documents, but I am not interested in complex semantic tagging. I could create a functional pipeline that privileges the simplest data and publishing model by transcribing my documents in Markdown and serving up all of the texts in a static website. Those minimal transcriptions could be downloaded as .html files and easily transformed into any format (including TEI Lite) using the conversion tool Pandoc.[210] What minimal computing suggests is that instead of creating rich, semantically encoded documents first, editors could instead focus on first creating a minimum viable product, which they could share and results-test in a publishable format; semantic encoding would be a further step, should the project gain more resources. But pragmatic editing also suggests that there is no law that all digital editions must use TEI – there are many good reasons to use Omeka, Scalar, Digital Mappa, or WordPress if one of those platforms effectively publishes the scholarship.

Modelling editions as archives of experience requires a balanced approach of creating vocabularies and tools, and a complementarity between print and digital texts, deep knowledge and wide-ranging interconnected knowledge, and prosaic and aesthetic experiences. This amounts to a broader conception of the edition based on its contexts of use and readers' experiences with technologies ranging from the book to the data set. An example of such an approach is the Shakespeare Census, which features descriptions and links to all extant copies of all Shakespeare editions up to 1700.[211] The point of the Census is not to edit documents but to curate reliable, interlinked data about versions of extant texts. Publishing editions in the digital age requires editors to rethink our strategies for modelling projects, and to be more mindful of the resource constraints and access

---

[209] Gil's Ed theme for Jekyll (http://elotroalex.github.io/ed/) offers a prototype for publishing minimal editions

[210] Pandoc (https://pandoc.org) is a command line tool that performs universal document conversions.

[211] Hooks and Lesser, *Shakespeare Census*.

issues that we face. This situation has not always entailed opportunities for new interpretations; Alan Blackwell characterised it as 'a mechanism of instruction'.[212] What is the data of an edition supposed to do, then, and what kinds of experience can the computer facilitate? Amy Earhart has argued that, despite the advantages of digital editions, most early attempts 'did not provide proof for the claim that digitization allows scholars to ask and answer new questions'.[213] One reason for this lack of insights was the attention given over to encoding those mechanisms of instruction otherwise known as book- or document-like metaphors (what Earhart calls the 'whole-text' approach), which, as Ted Nelson has been known to put it, merely simulate paper. Complementing code and pragmatic interpretation could enable new modes of analysis that allow us to 'study texts and works in editions that live in the digital medium' alongside reading in books, as Gabler suggests.[214] Computation should compound the insights and pleasures afforded by reading books. With these new modes of thinking come new possibilities of publication and hybridity through statistical and visualisation tools. However, publication has proven to be one of the most difficult aspects of the enterprise.

---

[212] Blackwell, 'What Does Digital Content Mean?' in Bardzell, Bardzell, and Blythe (eds.), *Critical Theory and Interaction Design*, p. 176. I am also grateful to Blackwell for speaking to me about this topic and suggesting the work of McCarthy and Wright.

[213] Earhart, *Traces of the Old, Uses of the New*, p. 12.

[214] Gabler, 'Theorizing the Digital Scholarly Edition', in *Text Genetics and Literary Modernism*.

5 Conclusion: The Challenges of Publishing Digital Editions

One of the most difficult aspects of digital research that is not discussed enough is that there are few good publishing solutions for digital scholarly editions. James Cummings, a long-standing member of the TEI Council, stated in a 2019 article that 'the publishing of a scholarly digital edition is still a needlessly complicated affair', even for a straightforward TEI project.[215] Most publications of scholarly editions and monographs on digital research still appear in print and e-book formats.

As of this writing (in late 2020), I know of only one general option for publishing a peer-reviewed digital scholarly edition using TEI XML markup: *Scholarly Editing* (https://scholarlyediting.org/), the annual for the Association for Documentary Editing. In my field of nineteenth-century literature, Romantic Circles (http://romantic-circles.org/editions) and COVE (https://editions.covecollective.org/) have created peer-reviewed publishing pipelines for digital editions. I applaud *Scholarly Editing* (and have been published in it twice), as well as Romantic Circles and COVE, but these publishing options are limited to smaller editions[216] of historical documents and period-specific texts, respectively, and they have limited interface options. Nor do they facilitate print publication. Other promising initiatives such as TEI Publisher, TAPAS, EFES, and PRISMS offer ready-made stylesheets for publishing web versions of TEI projects, but all come with disadvantages: some are difficult to set up, do not serve the interface needs of many projects, and do not have the peer review, distribution, marketing, and maintenance support that traditional publishers have.[217] As a result of these difficulties, several projects have resorted to using content management platforms such as Omeka, and, as I showed in Exhibition 2 in Section 3.2, the *Bow in the Cloud* project uses Scalar (and keeps a separate

---

[215] Cummings, 'Opening the Book', p. 190.

[216] *Scholarly Editing*'s model of the micro-edition is exemplary and should be pursued in several publishing contexts.

[217] TEI Publisher: https://teipublisher.com/index.html; TAPAS: https://tapasproject.org/; PRISMS: www.prisms.digital/; EFES (https://github.com/EpiDoc/EFES). See also Bodard and Yordanova, 'Publication, Testing and Visualization with EFES'.

GitHub repository for storing the Markdown and XML data). Being dependent on a platform still comes with disadvantages. MEL, on the other hand, uses a TEI workflow combining GitHub, CETEIcean,[218] Jekyll, and Netlify to publish a low-maintenance static website.

Many publishers are creating better workflows in the monograph space, but with limited data formats. For example, the Illinois Open Publishing Network (IOPN), under the Windsor & Downs Press imprint, publishes digital scholarly editions of literary works in the public domain. Like the IOPN, the Manifold publishing programme[219] has pioneered multimedia scholarly monographs. Publishers like these are offering well-supported, out-of-the-box content management tools for publishing open access born-digital projects (with separate data repositories in GitHub). Manifold has an impressive publishing pipeline that offers a variety of reading and engagement experiences that dovetail with much of my thinking. A minimal computing solution offered through programmes such as the Getty Publications Quire publishing tool shows the potential of creating sustainable resources, based on simple Markdown data models, for disseminating cultural heritage collections.[220] However, none of these publishing enterprises supports the rich semantic markup that TEI XML affords.

The current model for successful digital editions is to create a bespoke individual publishing system from the ground up, independently of a publisher, and to receive substantial support from grant funding, university IT departments, a supportive academic administration, dedicated staff, and a community of scholars willing to donate their labour. The tide seems to be changing with new initiatives such as the Mellon-NHPRC Digital Edition Publishing Cooperatives Program and its recent call for funding editions of ethnic minority projects. For now, though, the dearth of

---

[218] CETEIcean (https://teic.github.io/CETEIcean/), developed by Hugh Cayless, is a JavaScript library that allows TEI documents to be displayed in a Web browser dynamically by renaming the TEI elements in HTML (following Web Components standards). CETEIcean does not rely on an XSLT transformation within the browser, so it preserves the structure and information from a TEI data model.

[219] See https://manifoldapp.org/. [220] See https://quire.getty.edu/.

publication support for most digital editors means that a lot of promising small- to medium-sized projects have not been published, properly evaluated, or hosted on a sustainable and discoverable platform. Many students in my digital editing classes leave wondering how they will publish their individual projects – they have learned editorial methodologies and TEI markup, but what can they do with their data, and how will it benefit their careers? I have never been able to provide a better answer than the standard line – 'You should learn even more about XML technologies and web development and publish it yourself' – which is not a good answer for a busy graduate student or early career scholar. The graduate students and early career scholars who are typically the most eager to learn these new technologies are also the most precarious, so it is tone-deaf to suggest self-publication in an academic environment in which prestigious peer-reviewed print publications are still privileged for securing an open-ended contract or promotion. Nor can I say, 'Send your TEI XML file(s) to a university press for evaluation' because publishers will not currently accept that format. How could this be? One reason is that publishers continue to operate under a workflow that privileges book (and book-like) publication.

What is ironic is that we are already employing a digital workflow when we submit to a publisher, as we submit printer's copy via digital delivery of an electronic word processor file. Development of databases, content management systems, and digital content delivery has been underway in academic publishing since the mid-1980s, yet the current practice is ambivalent, if not hostile, towards open access data formats.[221] Most publishers use proprietary digital tools to publish analogue books and articles first, so the digital publication formats merely reflect the form of the book or journal article. Such a process makes a born-digital edition even more difficult to accomplish. Much of my time digital editing at the Mark Twain Project was spent encoding already published print books of the Works into TEI XML, which would then be transformed into HTML display. Even with so-called simultaneous print and digital publication, we were publishing print books first, then tediously re-engineering those

---

[221] Thompson, *Books in the Digital Age*, pp. 312–18.

books into electronic editions on the website.[222] What resulted was less a digital edition and more of a digital copy of the book with hyperlinks and pop-up notes.

A better digital publication workflow would focus on creating FAIR data first, rather than being driven by book-like outputs. The files of record would be open-source interoperable data files (plain text (.txt), Markdown (.md), HTML, XHTML, epub, or TEI XML), which would then be delivered to the publisher, then an interface would be created for its digital tools and interfaces in addition to its creation of a book design template. The reason why this solution has not been widely accepted is twofold: many scholars are still uncomfortable with creating TEI XML documents, and publishers do not accept TEI XML files because they do not have the publishing workflow set up for the ingestion of bespoke data models (even a Microsoft Word file has an underlying XML data model, but it is consistent across all types of files and has publication support).

This publication crux reinforces a feature of TEI XML that is also problematic: XML is extensible (i.e., flexible) and semantic (i.e., not presentational), so it requires transformation in order to be serviceable for modern Web browsers and other reading formats. Presentational data is geared towards a specific display interface, whereas semantic data is for archiving purposes, irrespective of any particular interface. The transformation scenario underscores a difference between technological layers of implementation (an applied programming problem) and layers of interpretation (an epistemological problem) of the scholarly annotations in the XML data. Publishers could hire developers to work with editors to transform these layers into a digital edition for the Web, but the complex nature of many TEI projects is such that each project requires a human being to interpret the encoding and editorial decisions and to create bespoke stylesheets to render their features. Without significant support, many digital scholarly editors are expected to serve in nearly every publishing and technical role: they are doing not just the intellectual work that goes into the editing but also the typesetting (markup), the publishing platform

---

[222] One exception (among others no doubt): the Letters section of Mark Twain Project Online now employs a born digital workflow.

(interface), the distribution PDF (data or web server), and the maintenance of the edition. This scenario will never be efficient at scale. This is why some have suggested that we are in the midst of a digital incunable phase – you might call it the first infancy of the digital art, using a new technology to manually typeset new representations of texts.[223] But this situation also recalls the inefficiencies in printing and publishing before the Industrial Revolution – that is, before the technologies such as the Stanhope (c.1800) and Koenig (c.1811) presses were invented to reduce the manual labour involved in hand press printing. Printing and publishing have always been driven by speed and scale – this is just as true for nineteenth-century newspapers and magazines as it is for modern-day HTML-based websites (and, in the case of scholarly publishing, articles and reference resources).

One of the most sizeable collections of digital editions, Oxford Scholarly Editions Online (OSEO; www.oxfordscholarlyeditions.com/), exemplifies this publication crux. OSEO, starting in around 2008, sought to create what Rupert Mann of Oxford University Press (OUP) described to me as 'a virtuous circle' to attract other editions.[224] The way OUP saw it, the fewer platforms, the better, which is why OSEO adopted similar technologies as those used in their monographs platform, Oxford Scholarship Online. The conversions of OUP editions into OSEO were still digital representations of already published books and came with an additional constraint that they could not be re-edited for digital publication. OUP did consider using TEI to encode the backlist, but TEI adoption would have required a reinvention of each edition and constituted a massive technical innovation for encoding books that were already edited. This kind of innovation is not just a matter of time, as an application of their existing schema was time-consuming enough; there was also the difficulty of such a large change for technical, editing, and publication staff. It was a practical decision to create their own in-house XML schema, similar to the one already in use for monographs, 'to minimise expensive novelty both in the data capture and in the publication technology', as Mann put it.

---

[223] Crane et al., 'Beyond Digital Incunabula'.

[224] Conversation with the author, 11 March 2019.

The development of OSEO raises a pertinent question for any digital publishing enterprise: how do we do data capture, and where are the data constraints going to come from, inside or outside of the publishing house? OSEO constrained from within the publishing house, as other publishers in books and journals have done, to maintain a consistent production pipeline. Mann and his colleagues working on OSEO agreed with the necessity of a born-digital workflow, but they also believed that TEI's complexity would prove to be disproportionately expensive for digital publication of existing print editions. What's the value that could be put on TEI adoption?

A similar set of problems came up in a different publishing context – the notable open access publisher OpenBook in the UK. OpenBook's co-director Rupert Gatti explained to me what he saw as the longevity problem of putting books online without sufficient support.[225] OpenBook was also intrigued by TEI, and was broadly supportive of born-digital publications. As Gatti suggested, one ideal of publishing is to make sure that books are available in 150 years; one cannot do that with digital editions, but with a book you can publish the material thing and walk away. Books and digital media still require maintenance and support. Books may last for 150 years, but not if they are left in a field. Most academic books will be read by small audiences after they are printed and are not likely to be read after a few decades. It may be beside the point to desire a book to be citable in 150 years' time. Instead, it is better to concentrate on making the edition data available to peers and the public now. In this respect, OpenBook has undoubtedly succeeded.

The expense of a digital platform is significant, whereas maintenance expenses for books are still low, although there are still costs for storage space and cataloguing of print books. The average 'first copy' production costs for each book at OpenBook is just over £5,000 per title (and printing 1.1 p per page), whereas hosting and maintenance costs for an interactive

---

[225] Conversation with the author, 28 March 2019.

website could be several thousand pounds per year.[226] It is still cheaper to publish books than it is to publish e-books and websites, which require encoders to test the validity of the underlying markup, servers to store the data, and IT staff. Unlike OSEO, which is a subscription service, OpenBook publishes free downloadable files in various formats (including XML), and offers a print-on-demand service, which is laudable and does allow people to take possession of the works in multiple formats. As John Thompson has shown, the digital revolution did not kill off the book, it 'gave it a new lease of life' because publishers like OpenBook can now host books in a 'virtual warehouse' and pay the costs of printing only when a book order has been requested.[227] Data presentation is still another challenging, and unresolved, matter. The problem with a TEI XML workflow, according to Gatti, is that it still does not have a typesetter in XML that is good enough for scalable print and web conversions.

Why would an editor publish TEI-based editions when it is not a widely adopted method of XML data entry and typesetting in the publishing industry? Most readers still want the print product, even now; very few customers are demanding XML from the publisher. The Web application is an engagement tool, but it is not as popular as a reading tool. TEI XML editing does not currently scale – to scale would require publishers to automate the process of transforming the XML, but automation would risk flattening out the individual features of each project. Scholarly publishing has tended to use the JATS and BITS XML schemas for journals and books, respectively, which are derived from the National Library of Medicine (NLM) standard originally created by Elsevier (and given the imprimatur of the National Information Standards Organization). These schemas usually work in parallel with an Adobe InDesign workflow for PDF and epub production. The result of these much more constrained XML schemas is that humanities scholarly publishing has followed a science-initiated workflow, contributing in part to the lack of adequate functionality that disadvantages literary editing projects. Also, as OSEO demonstrated, the model of publication still follows a monographic format.

---

[226] See Barnes and Gatti, 'The Cost of Open Access Books'.

[227] Thompson, *Book Wars*, pp. 12–15.

There is also no substantial market for TEI-encoded content that people want credit for publishing. Making data available online for other digital scholars could enable all kinds of experiences and possibilities; however, getting credit for digital editing projects is still a challenge in the academic politics of hiring and promotion.

Nobody I spoke to in the publishing industry denied the importance of digital editions and the TEI, yet they also admitted that the material on the computer screen is evanescent, and that people want stable resources. The goal for any digital editor or publisher, to echo Katherine Bode, is to create 'a stable and accessible representation of a historical literary system for others to investigate'.[228] Scholarly publishers could meet this challenge by accommodating a simplified set of stylesheets to render TEI Lite submissions, build up more complicated stylesheets from there as more projects come in, and make sure to create persistent DOIs for the edition data set.[229] But publishers face the same resource constraints as university libraries, so they need to create efficiencies. It would be too easy to blame publishers for their ambivalence towards born-digital workflows and bespoke digital projects. Many of them are aware of the problem and wish they could fix it. One of the understandable reasons for the hesitancy of publishers is that many of them do not know what a digital edition is, and the functionality and uses of digital editions have not been sufficiently explained and demonstrated to them by the academics producing them. The complex current TEI guidelines provide little clarity. Complex digital projects are never 'finished' like a book is; even if they are completed, updates to content and maintenance will still incur costs. The technical know-how for creating digital editions now is sometimes so complex and layered that a project requires one or more skilled software developers to untangle its encoding system and to create a workable interface, as well as systems administrators to look after the resource. A plethora of bespoke editions is not cost-effective for publishers.

---

[228] See Bode, 'The Equivalence of "Close" and "Distant" Reading'.

[229] TEI Lite (https://tei-c.org/guidelines/customization/lite/) is a simplified subset of TEI elements that accommodates most project needs.

What, then, is the meaning and function of the publisher in the digital age? It has become a company that provides a service: it arranges typesetting, peer review (sometimes), proofreading, printing, marketing and distribution, and digital information management. It can also be a public service that publishes reliable academic work. Yet journal and book publishing among the major players aims for volume and reducing costs. Academic publishing was ahead of the curve in the move to digital in the early 2000s: owing to their specialist topics and low expected print runs (and high price points), academic book publishers were among the first to move away from offset to digital printing. The publishing professionals transforming the scholarly files are not typically qualified to judge the content, and the scholars submitting content are rarely qualified to work with the proprietary digital publishing systems. Academic publishers have been disinvesting on book publishing and focusing more on digital systems to disseminate shorter resources such as journal articles and reference material because they have more predictable data models and cash flows. Large publishers that do have vast books and journals programmes in humanities and social sciences are not gaining ground in the more lucrative fields of life and health sciences, so they have less incentive to invest in system development.

Businesses that create files for various online libraries run on similar systems. Because of co-operation across the industry to invest in software systems, as content needs to migrate smoothly across platforms, the costs of typesetting and book design have been reduced.[230] Technology in publishing is evolving at a rapid pace, yet that innovation by digital publishers and scholars is happening on parallel tracks, and this is hindering scholarly progress. From a publisher's point of view, the author should create the content, and the publisher should focus on the typesetting, preparation, and distribution. But many publishers outsource many of these activities, which contributes to the fragmentation of information and expertise. As soon as authors veer into publishing, technical tool development, or content management territory by creating, for example, their own typesetting or encoding vocabulary, they will make scalable publishing more difficult.

---

[230] For an indispensable survey of this 'hidden revolution' in digital publishing workflows, see Thompson, *Books in the Digital Age*, ch. 15.

Publishing platforms are not currently ready to display several semantic features that scholarly editors tend to care about (maps and network graphs, for example). Again, they need to have *scale* to justify the investment; at scale, each project costs less to produce.[231] Perhaps these quandaries mean that publishers will play less of a role in the making of scholarly editions going forward, but that also puts the onus on the individual scholar, or small team of scholars, to raise the money required to publish and maintain them.

Another challenge for publishing digital editions is long-term preservation of scholarly data. The University of Victoria's Endings Project (https:// endings.uvic.ca/) illustrates one kind of solution that is 'creating tools, principles, policies and recommendations for digital scholarship practitioners to create accessible, stable, long-lasting resources in the humanities'. In this respect, libraries are well placed to support digital editing projects and data archiving of editorial scholarship with centralised digital repositories, open-source tools, and community activities.[232] Paige Morgan, Head of Digital Scholarship and Publishing Services at the University of Delaware Library, noted similar problems to the ones with which publishers have struggled. Morgan said that most libraries have insufficient infrastructure and staff resources, and, despite the longevity of TEI, only a few institutions have the infrastructure to steadily produce TEI-encoded scholarly editions and other bespoke digital projects.[233] Few academics have access to XSLT and web developers in their library or IT departments. The TEI community is not always forthright about the labour, time, and resources required for the sustainability and infrastructure of digital projects. Larger academic and administrative communities are less cognisant of the labour involved, which is evident not only in the lack of library resources but also in the fact that contributors to digital and editorial projects tend to be early career scholars on fixed-term contracts or dependent on diminishing pots of grant funding. Many scholars lack 'technical research infrastructure'. Even if IT staff could

---

[231] I thank José Pedro Moreira, Platform Usability Manager at Wiley, for offering his knowledge of current publishing systems, in conversations from October 2020.

[232] Clement et al., 'Toward a Notion of the Archive of the Future'.

[233] Conversation with the author, 20 March 2019.

support digital projects, many of them are placed within one-size-fits-all managerial contexts of customer portals: they still need to devote their time to core IT services for the university, and some see humanities as too varied and scattered to merit being efficiently supported, or they will support projects only if they receive grant funding.

As I said, text encoding takes significant amounts of time, and digital researchers still struggle to maintain a balance between the technological and the scholarly resources required to do the work well. Because there are few plug-and-play digital edition projects, digital editors still spend too much time learning and teaching tools, markup, and programming languages to potential contributors to the field and not enough time on the practices – or the concepts – of editing. Andrew Goldstone suggests that teachers of digital methods spend insufficient time analysing data 'to argue *with* data'.[234] Yet it remains a problem, as I said in the Introduction, that TEI XML workshops spend most of their energy teaching a markup language without showing you how to analyse *why* the text is being edited in a certain way, and *why* a TEI vocabulary is sufficient for the task at hand. Rather than perpetuating the idea that students *should* be able to learn a markup and/or programming language in a few sessions or a semester, we should frame the limits of what can be taught in short-term formats and give students and colleagues a general knowledge of general markup concepts as an appropriate base. The thinking tools of the editor-bibliographer would dictate the reasons why – and whether – TEI XML is appropriate, and the technologically literate pragmatist would then consider what experiences the edition is facilitating.

The academic norms of limited resources and labour imbalances remain in editing. Administrative leaders in publishing, libraries, and humanities departments could consider editing to be one of the most political acts in research: students and researchers editing and publishing underprivileged and neglected voices are a ballast against the still-dominant value of creating 'major' editions for canonical authors and political figures that take decades, and huge amounts of resources, to complete. More libraries are starting to focus on creating open-source publishing platforms using simple content

[234] See Goldstone, 'Teaching Quantitative Methods'.

management tools, such as Omeka and Scalar, for students and researchers across institutions. These kinds of initiative reinforce the nexus among digital research, archives, and libraries in promoting core competencies of humanities.

Again, greater support within university libraries may be the answer to getting around the publication and skills problems.[235] I saw this arrangement work out well when I worked for the Mark Twain Project Online, which was housed within the Bancroft Library and had the support of Berkeley's library IT system and the California Digital Library infrastructure. The *Bow in the Cloud* project, as it currently stands, would not have been possible without the John Rylands Research Institute's library infrastructure upgrades that integrated TEI and IIIF. Doubtless there are other libraries that are already making this happen (University of Michigan Press, for example, became a division of the UM University Libraries system, and the University of Virginia Center for Digital Editing and Rotunda Press co-operates with its library). In addition to calling for up-to-date research infrastructure, library staff have been lobbying for more teaching of technological fundamentals.[236] This has led to other community-driven digital education models such as library carpentry workshops, Wikipedia hackathons, and transcription co-creation hackathons of archival documents using tools such as Zooniverse and From the Page. Within these contexts, students can engage in problem-solving rather than only learning how to code. We need to reinforce the notion that a scholarly edition is curated data that need to be shared (as I said earlier, something you can take possession of). Within the library, editions could also provide subject guides to demonstrate how editions could be used in teaching situations. But with so many digital editions effectively functioning as independent, bespoke publishing projects, discovery is still a challenge.

A 2018 survey on the state of digital manuscript-based editions and tool development substantiates many of the shortcomings I have encountered in

---

[235] For a good model, see the programme at New York University elucidated in Vinopal and McCormick, 'Supporting Digital Scholarship in Research Libraries'.

[236] For an excellent blueprint for such teaching methods, see Blaney et al., *Doing Digital History*.

my own practice (I did not respond to the survey as I was not aware of it at the time).[237] The results emphasise the importance of producing tool-independent data, and creating intellectual 'trading zones' among technologists, scholars, librarians, and curators. Their piece reflects a recent 'concern that the existing digital infrastructure and tools for manuscript studies are failing to address the wide range of workflows, use cases, and research and pedagogical needs of scholars and curators in the field. Some of these issues arise from technological barriers'. Scholars desire better collaboration, smart workflows, and the integration of text and image data – as well as the easy ability to annotate the text and image data. Curators and technologists seem to want more integration, attention to metadata, and reliable standards. In many ways, IIIF accomplishes all of these, but IIIF is still challenging for institutions to set up and its associated tools (such as Project Mirador) still do not offer the full range of functionality that many editors require. Despite the efforts of many digital practitioners, 'there is still no end-to-end [publishing] solution that meets the myriad needs of scholars, curators, librarians, and students', owing to the diverse needs of projects, funding barriers, and insufficient tools.

Another recent survey of digital editions showed that the most common issues of digital editions involve the lack of data reusability, interoperability, licensing, image availability, and detailed documentation.[238] The majority of respondents in both surveys are against data silos. Scholars build silos because there are few professional incentives for breaking out of them. In a university context of scarcity and diminishing faith in the value of the humanities, scholars exist in an environment of marketised incentives such as league tables, self-promotion, and research grant capture. With so few secure jobs in the humanities, scholars are not incentivised to be collaborative and share their work. The authors of both surveys make the case for more tool development, even though such development is often associated with a form of 'technical assistance' that is generally not rewarded as 'research' in academia. The majority of survey respondents want '[t]ools and workflows to create and publish digital scholarly editions

[237] Almas et al., 'Manuscript Study in Digital Spaces'.
[238] Franzini et al., 'Digital Editions of Text'.

of works (e.g., digital critical editions, multi-text editions), including peer-review mechanisms'. Such tools and processes are still lacking owing to the lack of pragmatism – especially of a clear sense of collective intentionality – on the part of scholars, technologists, and publishers to meet the moment with flexible systems of publication and research value.

The chapters in this book employ pragmatism to re-think editorial principles and modelling of digital scholarly editions. My overriding concern is to approach scholarly editing and digital publishing through the lens of experience, emphasising intersubjective and interpenetrating practices and experimentation – from passing theories of intentionality to encoding as text analysis to a pragmatic theory of editing and technology for publication. Moving from abstract-rationalist models to a programme of action and experimentation liberates editors to examine the use of their editions in various media. Such a programme also seeks to resist a still-dominant culture of innovation at all costs[239] that runs the risk of replicating the off-putting and exclusionary tendencies of Big Theory with the libertarian ethos of Big Tech by implying that only well-resourced projects can be successful.[240] Experimentation does not necessarily mean creating the most innovative tool; rather, it is about giving readers the freedom to engage with texts in a meaningful and creative way. We need to demonstrate the excitement of creating and maintaining basic knowledge resources and choosing the public benefit over prestige metrics and income streams. I also need to return to the themes of invention and intentionality that were developed in the Introduction and Chapter 2. Chapters 3 and 4 also build on the intentional relations inherent in data and edition productions, capturing the intersubjective dynamism of authors, texts, editors, readers, and media that is crucial to the enterprise of inventive editing. Authorial intention undergirds a pragmatic editorial policy, but those intentions must then be projected onto and agreed upon by a collective of scholars and

---

[239] In *The Innovation Delusion*, Vinsel and Russell make a powerful argument about the dangers of 'innovation speak', and how pursuing novelty for its own sake fuels inequality, exhausts resources, and distracts from the crucial activities of maintenance and repair.

[240] Pannapacker, 'Digital Humanities Triumphant?'.

publishers working in tandem as they test, revise, and improve upon previous editorial work. The basic idea of collective intentionality is for groups to be *jointly directed* at objects (editions of works) and goals (open data).

Putting philosophy and praxis into dialogue, I contend that publishing scholarly data should be the primary aim of editors – data that can facilitate various reading and aesthetic experiences of editions that can cope with the inevitable changes in technology. Yet these editorial exhibitions also need to be activated and mediated, which makes open access, accessibility, and instrumental experimentation even more crucial – that is, releasing different file formats for different experiences allows the reader to possess and manipulate them for their own aims. Data still requires interfaces, but even a minimal computing approach can offer interfaces for presentation, PDFs for reading, as well as data repositories that can be uploaded into existing visualisation and data mining tools. Editions, reimagined as exhibitions of works with multifaceted functions, and with several publishing options from a computational pipeline (including books), enable a variety of intellectual and aesthetic experiences. If publications are reconceived as pragmatic inventions based on reliable data collections, then editing can embrace the critical, aesthetic, and experimental potentialities within editions of experience.

References

Ahnert, R., Ahnert, S. E., Coleman, C., and Weingart, S. B., *The Network Turn* (Cambridge University Press, 2020).

Almas, B., Khazraee, E., Miller, M. T., and Westgard, J., 'Manuscript Study in Digital Spaces: The State of the Field and New Ways Forward', *Digital Humanities Quarterly* 12.2 (2018), http://digitalhumanities.org:8081/dhq/vol/12/2/000374/000374.html.

Amis, K., *Lucky Jim* (Penguin, 2000).

Andrews, T., 'The Third Way', *Variants* 10 (2013), 61–76.

Anscombe, E., *Intention* (Oxford University Press, 1957).

Antonini, A., Benatti, F., and Blackburn-Daniels, S., 'On Links To Be', 31st ACM Conference on Hypertext and Social Media (13–15 July 2020), Online, http://oro.open.ac.uk/70781/1/on%20links%20to%20be.pdf.

Aristotle, *Rhetoric*, ed. W. D. Ross (Clarendon Press, 1959), accessed on the Perseus Digital Library, ed. G. R. Crane, www.perseus.tufts.edu/hopper/text?doc=urn:cts:greekLit:tlg0086.tlg038.

Audi, R. (ed.), 'Ontological commitment', in *The Cambridge Dictionary of Philosophy* (Cambridge University Press, 1999).

Bardzell J., Bardzell, S., and Blythe, M. A. (eds.), *Critical Theory and Interaction Design* (MIT Press, 2018).

Barnes, L., and Gatti, R., 'The Cost of Open Access Books: A Publisher Writes' (28 May 2020), http://doi.org/10.11647/OBP.0173.0143.

Berners-Lee, T., 'Hypertext and Our Collective Destiny' (1995), www.w3.org/Talks/9510_Bush/Talk.html.

Berners-Lee, T., 'Linked Data', www.w3.org/DesignIssues/LinkedData.html.

Bernstein, R. J., *The Pragmatic Turn* (Polity Press, 2010).

Beshero-Bondar, E., and Donovan-Condron, K., 'Modelling Mary Russell Mitford's Networks', in A. O. Winckles and A. Rehbein (eds.), *Women's Literary Networks and Romanticism* (Liverpool University Press, 2018).

Blackburn, S., *Truth* (Profile, 2017).

Blackwell, A., 'What Does Digital Content Mean? Umberto Eco and *The Open Work*', in Bardzell, Bardzell, and Blythe (eds.), *Critical Theory and Interaction Design*, pp. 167–86.

Blaney, J., Milligan, S., Steer, M., and Winters, J., *Doing Digital History: A Beginner's Guide to Working with Text as Data* (University of Manchester Press, 2021).

Bodard, G., and Stoyanova, S., 'Epigraphers and Encoders: Strategies for Teaching and Learning Digital Epigraphy', in G. Bodard and M. Romanello (eds.), *Digital Classics Outside the Echo-Chamber* (Ubiquity Press, 2016), doi: https://doi.org/10.5334/bat.

Bodard, G., and Yordanova, P., 'Publication, Testing and Visualization with EFES: A Tool for All Stages of the EpiDoc XML Editing Process', *Digitalia* 65.1 (2020), https://doi.org/10.24193/subbdigitalia .2020.1.02.

Bode, K., 'The Equivalence of "Close" and "Distant" Reading; or, Toward a New Object for Data-Rich Literary History', *Modern Language Quarterly* 78.1 (2017), 77–106.

Bode, K., *Reading by Numbers* (Anthem, 2012).

Bode, K., 'Why You Can't Model Away Bias', *Modern Language Quarterly* 81.1 (2020), 95–124.

Bordalejo, B., 'Digital versus Analogue Textual Scholarship or The Revolution Is Just in the Title', *Digital Philology: A Journal of Medieval Cultures* 7.1 (Spring 2018), 7–28.

Bowers, F., *Bibliography and Textual Criticism* (Clarendon, 1964).

Bowles, P., *Conversations with Paul Bowles*, ed. G. Caponi (University Press of Mississippi, 1993).

Box, G. E. P., and Luceño, A., *Statistical Control: By Monitoring and Feedback Adjustment* (John Wiley & Sons, 1997).

Brandom, R., *Between Saying and Doing: Toward an Analytic Pragmatism* (Oxford University Press, 2008).

Brentano, F., *Psychologie vom empirischen Standpunkt* [*Psychology from an Empirical Standpoint*] (Duncker & Humblot, 1874).

Brooks, G., *To Disembark* (Third World Press, 1981).

Brown, D., 'William Lloyd Garrison, Transatlantic Abolitionism and Colonisation in the Mid Nineteenth Century: The Revival of the Peculiar Solution?', *Slavery and Abolition* 33.2 (2012), 233–50.

Browne, T., *A True and Full Coppy of That Which Was Most Imperfectly and Surreptitiously Printed Before under the Name of: Religio Medici* (London, 1643).

Bryant, J., 'Editing Melville in Manuscript', *Leviathan* 21.2 (June 2019), 107–32.

Bryant, J., *The Fluid Text: A Theory of Revision and Editing for Book and Screen* (University of Michigan Press, 2002).

Bryant, J., *Melville Unfolding: Sexuality, Politics, and the Versions of* Typee (University of Michigan Press, 2008).

Bryant, J., Kelley, W., and Ohge, C. (eds.), *Versions of* Billy Budd, Sailor, *Melville Electronic Library* (2019), https://melville.electroniclibrary.org /versions-of-billy-budd.html.

Burrows, J. F., *Computation into Criticism* (Oxford University Press, 1987).

Burrows, J. F., 'Textual Analysis', in S. Schreibman, R.Siemens, and J. Unsworth (eds.), *A Companion to Digital Humanities* (Blackwell, 2004), www.digitalhumanities.org/companion/.

Bushell, S., *Text as Process: Creative Composition in Wordsworth, Tennyson and Emily Dickinson* (University of Virginia Press, 2009).

Carroll, N., 'Interpretation and Intention: The Debate between Hypothetical and Actual Intentionalism', *Metaphilosophy* 31.1–2 (January 2000), 75–95.

Clement, T., Hagenmaier, W., and Knies, J. L., 'Toward a Notion of the Archive of the Future: Impressions of Practice by Librarians, Archivists, and Digital Humanities Scholars', *Library Quarterly* 83.2 (April 2013), 112–30.

Craig, E., *Knowledge and the State of Nature: An Essay in Conceptual Synthesis* (Oxford University Press, 1990).

Cramer, J. S. (ed.), *The Portable Emerson* (Penguin, 2014).

Crane, G., Bamman, D., Cerrato, L., Jones, A., Mimno, D., Packel, A., Sculley, D., and Weaver, G., 'Beyond Digital Incunabula: Modeling the Next Generation of Digital Libraries', *Proceedings of the 10th European Conference on Digital Libraries* (2006), Perseus Project, Tufts, 353–66, http://hdl.handle.net/10427/36131.

Crossley-Holland, K. (trs.), *The Exeter Book Riddles* (Enitharmon Press, 2008).

Crymble, A., 'Digital Library Search Preferences amongst Historians and Genealogists: British History Online User Survey', *Digital Humanities Quarterly* 10.4 (2016), www.digitalhumanities.org/dhq/vol/10/4/000270/000270.html.

Crymble, A., *Technology and the Historian: Transformations in the Digital Age* (University of Illinois Press, 2021).

Cummings, J., 'Opening the Book: Data Models and Distractions in Digital Scholarly Editing', *International Journal of Digital Humanities* (July 2019), 179–93, https://doi.org/10.1007/s42803-019-00016-6.

Daniels, J., and Thistlethwaite, P., 'Being a Scholar in the Digital Era', in J. Daniels and P. Thistlethwaite, *Transforming Scholarly Practice for the Public Good* (Policy Press, 2016).

Dasenbrock, R. W. (ed.), *Literary Theory after Davidson* (Pennsylvania State University Press, 1993).

Davidson, D., *Essential Davidson* (Oxford University Press, 2006).

Davidson, D., *Truth, Language, and History* (Oxford University Press, 2005).

Davie, D., *Essex Poems: 1963–1967* (Routledge & Kegan Paul, 1969).

Dekker, R., Bleeker, E., Buitendijk, B., Kulsdom, A., and Birnbaum, D., 'TAGML: A Markup Language of Many Dimensions', in *Proceedings of Balisage: The Markup Conference 2018* 21 (2018), DOI: https://doi.org/10.4242/BalisageVol21.HaentjensDekker01.

Deppmann, J., Ferrer, D., and Groden, M. (eds.), *Genetic Criticism: Texts and Avant-textes* (University of Pennsylvania Press, 2004).

Dewey, J., *Art as Experience* (Penguin, 2005).

Dewey, J., *Human Nature and Conduct* (Modern Library, 1922).

Dewey, J., *The Middle Works, 1899–1924, Volume 6: 1910–1911*, ed. J. A. Boydston (Southern Illinois University Press, 1978).

Dewey, J., *The Philosophy of John Dewey*, ed. J. McDermott (University of Chicago Press, 1973).

Drucker, J. 'Humanities Approaches to Graphical Display', *Digital Humanities Quarterly* 5.1 (2011), http://digitalhumanities.org/dhq/vol/5/1/000091/000091.html.

Earhart, A., *Traces of the Old, Uses of the New* (University of Michigan Press, 2015).

Eco, U., '*The Open Work* (1989)', trans. Anne Cancogni, in Bardzell, Bardzell, and Blythe (eds.), *Critical Theory and Interaction Design*, pp. 145–66.

Edel, L. (ed.) *Henry James: The Selected Letters* (Harvard University Press, 1987).

Eggert, P., *Securing the Past* (Cambridge University Press, 2009).

Empson, W., *Seven Types of Ambiguity* (New Directions, 1966).

Eve, M., *Close Reading with Computers: Textual Scholarship, Computational Formalism, and David Mitchell's* Cloud Atlas (Stanford University Press, 2019).

Ezell, M. J. M., 'Editing Early Modern Women's Manuscripts: Theory, Electronic Editions, and the Accidental Copy-Text', *Literature Compass* 7.2 (2010), 102–9.

Fazi, M. B., *Contingent Computation: Abstraction, Experience, and Indeterminacy in Computational Aesthetics* (Rowman and Littlefield, 2018).

Felski, R., *The Limits of Critique* (University of Chicago Press, 2015).

Ferguson, M., *Subject to Others: British Women Writers and Colonial Slavery, 1670–1834* (Routledge, 1992; 2014 reprint).

Franzini, G., Terras, M., and Mahony, S., 'Digital Editions of Text: Surveying User Requirements in the Digital Humanities', *Journal on Computing and Cultural Heritage* (February 2019), https://doi.org/10.1145/3230671.

Gabler, H. W., *Text Genetics and Literary Modernism* (OpenBook Publishers, 2018), https://doi.org/10.11647/OBP.0120.

Garcia, T. S., 'Working Together: The Digital World and English Studies', English Association Blog, 25 February 2019, www2.le.ac.uk/offices/english-association/news-1/working-together-the-digital-world-and-english-studies-by-tiago-sousa-garcia.

Gaskell, P., *A New Introduction to Bibliography* (Oak Knoll Press, 1978).

Gil, A., 'How (and Why) to Generate a Static Website Using Jekyll, Part 1', *Chronicle of Higher Education*, 31 August 2015, www.chronicle.com/blogs/profhacker/jekyll1/60913.

Gitelman, L. (ed.), *"Raw Data" Is an Oxymoron* (MIT Press, 2013).

Goldstone, A., 'Teaching Quantitative Methods: What Makes It Hard (in Literary Studies)', *Debates in the Digital Humanities* (2018), https://doi.org/doi:10.7282/T3G44SKG.

Grafton, A., *Inky Fingers: The Making of Books in Early Modern Europe* (Harvard University Press, 2020).

Greenberg, S., *A Poetics of Editing* (Palgrave Macmillan, 2018).

Greetham, D. C. (ed.), *Scholarly Editing: A Guide to Research* (Modern Language Association of America, 1995).

Greetham, D. C., 'Textual Forensics', *PMLA* 111.1 (January 1996), 32–51, https://doi.org/10.2307/463132.

Greetham, D. C., *Textual Scholarship: An Introduction* (Garland, 1994).

Greetham, D. C., *Theories of the Text* (Oxford University Press, 1999).

Greg, W. W., 'The Rationale of Copy-Text', *Studies in Bibliography* 3 (1950–1), 19–36.

Grice, H. P., *Studies in the Way of Words* (Harvard University Press, 1989).

Grimstad, P., *Experience and Experimental Writing: Literary Pragmatism from Emerson to the Jameses* (Oxford University Press, 2013).

Hancher, M., 'Three Kinds of Intention', *Modern Language Notes* 87 (December 1972), 827–51.

Hannon, M., *What's the Point of Knowledge?* (Oxford University Press, 2019).

Hirst, R., 'The Making of *The Innocents Abroad*: 1867–1872' (PhD diss., University of California, Berkeley, 1975).

Hooks, A. G., and Lesser, Z. (eds.), *Shakespeare Census* (created 2018). www.shakespearecensus.org.

Housman, A. E., 'The Application of Thought to Textual Criticism', *Proceedings of the Classical Association* 18 (London, 1921), 67–84.

Howard-Hill, T. H., 'W. W. Greg as Bibliographer', *Textual Cultures* 4.2 (Autumn 2009), 63–75.

Huzzey, R., *Freedom Burning: Anti-Slavery and Empire in Victorian Britain* (Cornell University Press, 2012).

Hyman, W., 'The Inner Lives of Renaissance Machines', in K. Curran (ed.), *Renaissance Personhood: Materiality, Taxonomy, Process* (Edinburgh University Press, 2020), 44–61.

James, W., and McDermott, J. J. (ed.), *The Writings of William James: A Comprehensive Edition* (University of Chicago Press, 1977).

Jockers, M., *Macroanalysis* (University of Illinois Press, 2013).

Jockers, M., *Text Analysis with R for Students of Literature* (Springer, 2014).

Kestenbaum, V., *The Grace and Severity of the Ideal: John Dewey and the Transcendent* (University of Chicago Press, 2002).

Lamarque, P., 'Wittgenstein, Literature, and the Idea of a Practice', *British Journal of Aesthetics* 50 (2010), 375–88.

Lamarque, P., *Work and Object* (Oxford University Press, 2010).

Lavagnino, J., 'Access', *Literary and Linguistic Computing* 24.1 (2009), 63–76, https://doi.org/10.1093/llc/fqn038.

Maes, H., 'Intention, Interpretation, and Contemporary Visual Art', *British Journal of Aesthetics* 50.2 (April 2010), 121–38.

Manns, J., 'Intentionalism in John Dewey's Aesthetics', *Transactions of the Charles S. Peirce Society* 23.3 (Summer, 1987), 411–23.

McCarthy, J., and Wright, P., *Technology as Experience* (MIT Press, 2004).

McCarty, W., 'Modelling the Actual, Simulating the Possible', in J. Flanders and F. Jannidis (eds.), *The Shape of Data in Digital Humanities: Modeling Texts and Text-Based Materials* (Routledge, 2018).

McDaniel, C., *The Problem of Democracy in the Age of Slavery: Garrisonian Abolitionists and Transatlantic Reform* (Louisiana State University Press, 2013).

McGann, J., *A Critique of Modern Textual Criticism* (University of Virginia Press, 1992).

McGann, J., *A New Republic of Letters* (Harvard University Press, 2014).

McGann, J., *Radiant Textuality: Literature after the World Wide Web* (Palgrave, 2001).

McKenzie, D. F., *Bibliography and the Sociology of Texts* (Cambridge University Press, 1999).

Melville, H., *Billy Budd, Sailor and Other Uncompleted Writings*, eds., H. Hayford, A. A. MacDougall, R. A. Sandberg, and G. T. Tanselle, Volume 13 of *The Writings of Herman Melville* (Northwestern University Press and the Newberry Library, 2017).

Melville, H., *The Piazza Tales and Other Prose Pieces, 1839–1860*, eds., H. Hayford, A. A. MacDougall, and G. T. Tanselle, Volume 9 of *The*

Writings of Herman Melville (Northwestern University Press and The Newberry Library, 1987).

Melville, H., *Typee: A Peep at Polynesian Life*, eds., H. Hayford, H. Parker, and G. T. Tanselle, Volume 1 of *The Writings of Herman Melville* (Northwestern University Press and the Newberry Library, 1968).

Menand, L., *Discovering Modernism: T. S. Eliot and His Context* (Oxford University Press, 2007).

Menand, L. (ed.), *Pragmatism: A Reader* (Vintage, 1997).

Milton, J., 'Areopagitica (1644)', in R. Flannagan (ed.), *The Riverside Milton* (Houghton Mifflin, 1998).

Misak, C., *Frank Ramsey: A Sheer Excess of Powers* (Oxford University Press, 2020).

Mole, T., *What the Victorians Made of Romanticism* (Princeton University Press, 2017).

Nelson, T., 'A Cosmology for a Different Computer Universe: Data Model, Mechanisms, Virtual Machine and Visualization Infrastructure', *Journal of Digital Information* 5.1 (2006). https://journals.tdl.org/jodi/index.php/jodi/article/view/131/129.

Ohge, C., 'Melville Incomplete', *American Literary History* 31.1 (Spring 2019), 139–50.

Ohge, C., 'Melville's Late Reading and the Revisions in the *Billy Budd* Manuscript', in B. Yothers (ed.), *Critical Insights: Billy Budd* (Salem Press, 2017), pp. 93–111.

Ohge, C., and Olsen-Smith, S., 'Digital Text Analysis at Melville's Marginalia Online', *Leviathan: A Journal of Melville Studies* 20.2 (2018), 1–16.

Ohge, C., and Tupman, C., 'Encoding and Analysis, and Encoding as Analysis, in Textual Editing', in S. Dunn and K. Schuster (eds.), *The Routledge International Handbook to Digital Humanities Research Methods*, ch. 17 (Routledge, 2020).

Ohge, C., Olsen-Smith, S., and Smith, E. B., with Brimhall, A., Howley, B., Shanks, L., and Smith, L., '"At the Axis of Reality": Melville's Marginalia in the Dramatic Works of William Shakespeare', *Leviathan: A Journal of Melville Studies* 20.2 (2018), 37–67.

Olsen-Smith, S., and Norberg, P. (eds.), *Melville's Marginalia Online*. http://melvillesmarginalia.org/.

Olsen-Smith, S., 'The Inscription of Walt Whitman's 'Live Oak, with Moss' Sequence: A Restorative Edition', *Scholarly Editing* 33 (2012), http://scholarlyediting.org/2012/editions/intro.liveoakwithmoss.html

Ozment, K., 'A Rationale for Feminist Bibliography', *Textual Cultures* 13.1 (2020), 149–78. DOI: 10.14434/textual.v13i1.30076.

Pannapacker, W., 'Digital Humanities Triumphant?' in M. K. Gold (ed.), *Debates in Digital Humanities* (University of Minnesota Press, 2012), https://doi.org/10.5749/9781452963754.

Parker, H., *Flawed Texts and Verbal Icons* (Northwestern University Press, 1984).

Parker, H., *Reading* Billy Budd (Northwestern University Press, 1990).

Pierazzo, E., *Digital Scholarly Editing: Theories, Models, and Methods* (Ashgate, 2015).

Piper, A., *Enumerations: Data and Literary Study* (University of Chicago Press, 2018).

Plato, *Parmenides*, in H. N. Fowler (ed. and trs.), *Plato in Twelve Volumes: With an English Translation, Cratylus, Parmenides, Greater Hippias, Lesser Hippias* (W. Heinemann, 1926), accessed on the Perseus Digital Library, ed. G. R. Crane, www.perseus.tufts.edu/hopper/text?doc=Perseus%3atext%3a1999.01.0174%3atext%3dParm.

Poirier, R., *Poetry and Pragmatism* (Faber and Faber, 1992).

Poirier, R., 'Why Do Pragmatists Want to Be Like Poets?', in M. Dickstein (ed.), *The Revival of Pragmatism* (Duke University Press, 1999), pp. 347–61.

Posner, M., and Klein, L. F., 'Editor's Introduction: Data as Media', *Feminist Media Histories* 3.3 (2017), 1–8, https://doi.org/10.1525/fmh.2017.3.3.1.

Price, L., *The Anthology and the Rise of the Novel: From Richardson to George Eliot* (Cambridge University Press, 2003).

Putnam, H., 'Philosophy and Our Mental Life', in H. Putnam (ed.), *Philosophical Papers, Volume 2: Mind, Language and Reality* (Cambridge University Press, 1975), pp. 291–303.

Putnam, H., *Pragmatism: An Open Question* (Blackwell, 1995).

Putnam, H., *Reason, Truth, and History* (Cambridge University Press, 1981).

Quine, W. V. O., *From a Logical Point of View: Nine Logico-philosophical Essays*, 2nd ed. (Harvard University Press, 1980).

Quine, W. V. O., *Philosophy of Logic* (Prentice-Hall, 1970).

Ramsey, S., 'The Hermeneutics of Screwing Around', in K. Kee (ed.), *Pastplay: Teaching and Learning History with Technology* (University of Michigan Press, 2014), pp. 111–30.

Rasmussen, K. S. G., 'Reading or Using a Digital Edition? Reader Roles in Scholarly Editions', in M. J. Driscoll and E. Pierazzo (eds.), *Digital Scholarly Editing: Theories and Practices* (OpenBook, 2016), http://dx.doi.org/10.11647/OBP.0095.07.

Ricks, C., *Essays in Appreciation* (Oxford University Press, 1996).

Ricks, C., 'In Theory', *London Review of Books* 3.7 (16 April 1981), 3–6.

Ricks, C., 'To Criticize the Critic', *Essays in Criticism* 69.4 (October 2019), 476, https://doi.org/10.1093/escrit/cgz021.

Rinard, S., 'Pragmatic Skepticism', *Philosophy and Phenomenological Research* (in press), www.susannarinard.com/s/Pragmatic-Skepticism-shhn.docx.

Robinson, P., 'Toward a Theory of Digital Editions', *Variants* 10 (2013), 105–31, https://doi.org/10.1163/9789401209021_009.

Rockwell, G., and Sinclair, S., *Hermeneutica* (MIT Press, 2016).

Rorty, R., *Consequences of Pragmatism* (University of Minnesota Press, 1982).

Rorty, R., *Contingency, Irony, and Solidarity* (Cambridge University Press, 1989).

Ryle, G., 'John Locke Re-edited', *Times Literary Supplement* (19 September 1975), p. 1043.

Sá Pereira, M. P., 'Mixed Methodological Digital Humanities', in M. K. Gold and L. F. Klein (eds.), *Debates in Digital Humanities* (University of Minnesota Press, 2019).

Scheinfeld, T., 'Sunset for Ideology, Sunrise for Methodology?', in M. K. Gold (ed.), *Debates in the Digital Humanities* (University of Minnesota Press, 2012), https://doi.org/10.5749/9781452963754.

Schloen, S., and Schloen, D., 'Beyond Gutenberg: Transcending the Document Paradigm in Digital Humanities', *Digital Humanities Quarterly* 8.4 (2014).

Searle, J., *Intentionality* (Cambridge University Press, 1983).

Searle, J. 'Reiterating the Differences: A Reply to Derrida', *Glyph* 1 (1977), 198–208.

Shakespeare, W., *Henry IV, Part I, The Arden Shakespeare*, ed. A. R. Humphreys (Methuen, 1965).

Shakespeare, W., *Richard III, The Arden Shakespeare*, ed. J. Siemon, 3rd ed. (Bloomsbury, 2009).

Shillingsburg, P., *From Gutenberg to Google* (Cambridge University Press, 2006).

Silge, J., and Robinson, D., *Text Mining with R: A Tidy Approach* (2020), www.tidytextmining.com/.

Smithies, J., *The Digital Humanities and the Digital Modern* (Palgrave Macmillan, 2017).

So, R. J., 'All Models Are Wrong', *PMLA* 132.3 (2017), 668–73.

Soames, S., 'Analytic Philosophy of Language', in K. Becker and I. Thomson (eds.), *The Cambridge History of Philosophy, 1945–2015* (Cambridge University Press, 2019). doi:10.1017/9781316779651.

Sperberg-McQueen, M., 'Representing Concurrent Document Structures Using Trojan Horse Markup', *Proceedings of Balisage: The Markup Conference*, Balisage Series on Markup Technologies, vol. 21 (2018), DOI: https://doi.org/10.4242/BalisageVol21.Sperberg-McQueen01.

Stockwell, P., and Mahlberg, M., 'Mind-Modelling with Corpus Stylistics in *David Copperfield*', *Language and Literature* 24. 2 (May 2015), 129–47, doi:10.1177/0963947015576168.

Tanselle, G. T., 'The Editorial Problem of Final Authorial Intention', *Studies in Bibliography* 29 (1976), 167–211.

Tanselle, G. T., 'Historicism and Critical Editing', *Studies in Bibliography* 39 (1986), 1–46.

Tanselle, G. T., 'Print History and Other History', *Studies in Bibliography* 48 (1995), 268–89.

Tanselle, G. T., *Rationale of Textual Criticism* (University of Pennsylvania Press).

Taylor, P., *Condition: The Ageing of Art* (Paul Holberton, 2015).

Thompson, J. B., *Books in the Digital Age: The Transformation of Academic and Higher Education Publishing in Britain and the United States* (Polity Press, 2005).

Thompson, J. B., *Book Wars: The Digital Revolution in Publishing* (Polity Press, 2021).

Thorpe, J., *Principles of Textual Criticism* (Huntington Library, 1972).

Underwood, T., *Distant Horizons* (University of Chicago Press, 2019).

Van Hulle, D., *Textual Awareness: A Genetic Study of Late Manuscripts by Joyce, Proust, and Mann* (University of Michigan Press, 2004).

Vinopal, J., and McCormick, M., 'Supporting Digital Scholarship in Research Libraries: Scalability and Sustainability', *Journal of Library*

Administration 53.1 (2013), 27–42, https://doi.org/10.1080/01930826.2013.756689.

Vinsel, L., and Russell, A., *The Innovation Delusion: How Our Obsession with the New Has Disrupted the Work That Matters Most* (Currency, 2020).

Waldman, D. (ed.), *Mark Rothko in New York* (Guggenheim Museum, 1994).

Weizenbaum, J., *Computer Power and Human Reason: From Judgement to Calculation* (W. H. Freeman and Company, 1976).

Wenke, J., 'Melville's Indirection: *Billy Budd*, the Genetic Text, and "the Deadly Space Between"', in D. Yannella (ed.), *New Essays on* Billy Budd (Cambridge University Press, 2002), pp. 114–44.

Werner, M. (ed.), *Writing In Time: Emily Dickinson's Master Hours* (Amherst College Press, 2021), p. 11, https://doi.org/10.3998/mpub.12023683.

Werstine, P., *Early Modern Playhouse Manuscripts and the Editing of Shakespeare* (Cambridge University Press, 2012).

Whitman, W., *Leaves of Grass* (New York, 1891), accessed at the Walt Whitman Archive, eds., M. Cohen, E. Folsom, and K. Price, https://whitmanarchive.org/published/LG/1891/poems/193.

Williams, S., *Data Action: Using Data for Public Good* (MIT Press, 2020).

Williams, W. P., and Abbott, C. S., *An Introduction to Bibliographical and Textual Studies*, 4th ed. (Modern Language Association of America, 2009).

Wimsatt, W. K., and Beardsley, M. C., 'The Intentional Fallacy', *Sewanee Review* 54.3 (1946), 468–88.

Wittgenstein, L., *Philosophical Investigations*, trans. G. E. M. Anscombe, 2nd ed. (Blackwell, 1997).

Wittgenstein, L., *Remarks on Colour* (Blackwell, 1977).

Wood, M., 'Radical Publishing', in M. F. Suarez, S.J. and M. L. Turner (eds.), *The Cambridge History of the Book in Britain, Volume 5: 1695–1830* (Cambridge University Press, 2009).

Woudhuysen, H. R. (ed.), *Samuel Johnson on Shakespeare* (Penguin, 1989).

Acknowledgements

This book would not have been possible without the support of my mentors. Jane Winters not only encouraged me to write this book but has also been a mentor to me since I arrived in London in 2017. Steven Olsen-Smith introduced me to Melville studies and trained me in graduate-level research methods when I was an undergraduate intern at *Melville's Marginalia Online*. He never wavered in his support for me, and his own extraordinary scholarly achievements spurred my explorations into Melville's creative process, bibliography, and digital research. Christopher Ricks, who co-directed the Editorial Institute with Archie Burnett when I was a student there, provided the haven I needed for my intellectual and creative aims as a graduate student; I could not have had a more generous and open-minded doctoral advisor and editorial mentor. Others at Boston University lent their expertise as I learned the craft of editing, particularly Marcia Karp and Frances Whistler.

Many ideas of this book started to germinate at the Mark Twain Papers & Project, where I worked under the direction of Robert Hirst and Harriet Elinor Smith between 2014–2017, and where I received a crash course in the practicalities of working on a major edition from several brilliant colleagues on the editorial staff. In London, I have continued to receive support from colleagues at the School of Advanced Study that made this project feasible. Clare Lees, Director of the Institute of English Studies since 2018, has been a resolute supporter. Other friends and colleagues in my scholarly community tested my ideas in this book over many stimulating conversations: Elisa Beshero-Bondar, David Birnbaum, Elli Bleeker, Gabriel Bodard, David Brown, James Cummings, Ronald Dekker, Tiago Sousa Garcia, Albert LaFarge, Nick Laiacona, Dennis Mischke, Leslie Myrick, Mathelinda Nabugodi, Andrew Nash, Elizabeth Savage, Simona Stoyanova, Charlotte Tupman, Elizabeth Williamson, Greg Woolf, and Mary Erica Zimmer. The work presented in Chapter 3 was made possible by a John Rylands Research Institute Digital Humanities Project Start-up Grant at the University of Manchester, and benefited from valuable advice from librarians Fran Baker and Jane Gallagher.

This book received significant feedback from several colleagues; any errors and infelicities are of course my own. I thank the anonymous peer reviewers for their detailed and helpful feedback. The copyeditor Lori Heaford significantly improved the text, not only catching several errors and cleaning up the citations but also suggesting many helpful revisions to improve clarity. Jonathan Blaney and Martin Steer graciously read the whole manuscript and offered excellent suggestions based on their digital expertise. John Bryant offered rigorous feedback on the whole manuscript, and I benefited from many follow-up conversations with him as we worked on MEL editions. Wyn Kelley read my Introduction and Chapters 2 and 4 and offered characteristically generous feedback. I am grateful to Simon Blackburn, Michael Hannon, and Barry C. Smith, all of whom gave their time to speak at length to me about the philosophical ideas in this book. The Conclusion also benefited from conversations with colleagues in the publishing and library sectors, to whom I am indebted for sharing their expertise: Rupert Gatti, Rupert Mann, José Pedro Moreira, and Paige Morgan. The book was also bolstered by working with colleagues on the forthcoming editorial Fundamentals course for the Institute of the Editing of Historical Documents: Neel Agrawal, Emily Bell, Katie Blizzard, Cathy Hajo, Jennifer Stertzer, and Serenity Sutherland. I also want to thank all my students in the MA in the History of the Book Programme at the Institute of English Studies; they have taught me as much as I tried to teach them, and discussions with them in seminars and supervisions enhanced this work.

I thank Jillian Saucier, who not only lent her editorial expertise to the whole manuscript but whose love and encouragement also helped me see this project through.

Kevin Crossley-Holland's Poem 51 from *The Exeter Book Riddles* is reproduced by permission of Enitharmon Press.

There has been substantial revision and augmentation of previous publications, as follows:

Section 2.2: 'Exhibition 1: Herman Melville's *Billy Budd, Sailor* (c.1886–1891)', deriving from 'Melville Incomplete', *American Literary History* 31.1 (Spring 2019), 139–50.

Section 3.1: 'Computation, Text Encoding, and Text Analysis', deriving from C. Ohge and C. Tupman, 'Encoding and Analysis, and Encoding as Analysis, in Textual Editing', in S. Dunn and K. Schuster (eds.), *The Routledge International Handbook of Research Methods in Digital Humanities*, ch. 17 (Routledge, 2020).

Cambridge Elements

Publishing and Book Culture

SERIES EDITOR
Samantha Rayner
University College London

Samantha Rayner is a Reader in UCL's Department of
Information Studies. She is also Director of UCL's Centre for
Publishing, co-Director of the Bloomsbury CHAPTER
(Communication History, Authorship, Publishing, Textual
Editing and Reading) and co-editor of the Academic Book of
the Future BOOC (Book as Open Online Content) with UCL
Press.

ASSOCIATE EDITOR
Leah Tether
University of Bristol

Leah Tether is Professor of Medieval Literature and Publishing
at the University of Bristol. With an academic background in
medieval French and English literature and a professional
background in trade publishing, Leah has combined her
expertise and developed an international research profile in
book and publishing history from manuscript to digital.

About the series

This series aims to fill the demand for easily accessible, quality texts available for teaching and research in the diverse and dynamic fields of Publishing and Book Culture. Rigorously researched and peer-reviewed Elements will be published under themes, or 'Gatherings'. These Elements should be the first check point for researchers or students working on that area of publishing and book trade history and practice: we hope that, situated so logically at Cambridge University Press, where academic publishing in the UK began, it will develop to create an unrivalled space where these histories and practices can be investigated and preserved.

Cambridge Elements ≡

Publishing and Book Culture

Academic Publishing

Gathering Editor: Jane Winters

Jane Winters is Professor of Digital Humanities at the School
of Advanced Study, University of London. She is co-convenor
of the Royal Historical Society's open-access monographs
series, New Historical Perspectives, and a member of the
International Editorial Board of Internet Histories and the
Academic Advisory Board of the Open Library of Humanities.

ELEMENTS IN THE GATHERING

A full series listing is available at: www.cambridge.org/EPBC